The Moon & Antarctica

Praise for the series:

It was only a matter of time before a clever publisher realized that there is an audience for whom *Exile on Main Street* or *Electric Ladyland* are as significant and worthy of study as *The Catcher in the Rye* or *Middlemarch* . . . The series . . . is freewheeling and eclectic, ranging from minute rock-geek analysis to idiosyncratic personal celebration—*The New York Times Book Review*

Ideal for the rock geek who thinks liner notes just aren't enough—*Rolling Stone*

One of the coolest publishing imprints on the planet—*Bookslut*

These are for the insane collectors out there who appreciate fantastic design, well-executed thinking, and things that make your house look cool. Each volume in this series takes a seminal album and breaks it down in startling minutiae. We love these. We are huge nerds—*Vice*

A brilliant series . . . each one a work of real love—*NME* (UK)

Passionate, obsessive, and smart—*Nylon*

Religious tracts for the rock 'n' roll faithful—*Boldtype*

[A] consistently excellent series—*Uncut* (UK)

We . . . aren't naive enough to think that we're your only source for reading about music (but if we had our way . . . watch out). For those of you who really like to know everything there is to know about an album, you'd do well to check out Bloomsbury's "33 1/3" series of books—*Pitchfork*

For almost 20 years, the 33-and-a-Third series of music books has focused on individual albums by acts well known (Bob Dylan, Nirvana, ABBA, Radiohead), cultish (Neutral Milk Hotel, Throbbing Gristle, Wire) and many levels in-between. The range of music and their creators defines "eclectic," while the writing veers from freewheeling to acutely insightful. In essence, the books are for the music fan who (as *Rolling Stone* noted) "thinks liner notes just aren't enough."—*The Irish Times*

For reviews of individual titles in the series, please visit our blog at 333sound.com and our website at https://www.bloomsbury.com/academic/music-sound-studies/

Follow us on Twitter: @333books
Like us on Facebook: https://www.facebook.com/33.3books
For a complete list of books in this series, see the back of this book.

Forthcoming in the series:

I'm Wide Awake, It's Morning by Holden Seidlitz
Re by Carmelo Esterrich
New Amerykah Part Two (Return of the Ankh) by Kameryn Alexa Carter
Tragic Kingdom by Rhae Lynn Barnes
Paris 1919 by Mark Doyle
Blue Bell Knoll by Chris Tapley

and many more . . .

The Moon & Antarctica

Zachary Petit

BLOOMSBURY ACADEMIC
NEW YORK • LONDON • OXFORD • NEW DELHI • SYDNEY

BLOOMSBURY ACADEMIC
Bloomsbury Publishing Inc
1385 Broadway, New York, NY 10018, USA
50 Bedford Square, London, WC1B 3DP, UK
29 Earlsfort Terrace, Dublin 2, Ireland

BLOOMSBURY, BLOOMSBURY ACADEMIC and the Diana logo are trademarks of
Bloomsbury Publishing Plc

First published in the United States of America 2024
Reprinted 2025 (twice)

Library of Congress Cataloging-in-Publication Data

Names: Petit, Zachary, author.
Title: The Moon & Antarctica / Zachary Petit.
Other titles: Modest Mouse's Moon & Antarctica | Moon and Antarctica
Description: [1.] | New York: Bloomsbury Academic, 2024. |
Series: 33 1/3 | Includes bibliographical references.
Identifiers: LCCN 2024019622 (print) | LCCN 2024019623 (ebook) |
ISBN 9798765106754 (paperback) | ISBN 9798765106761 (ebook) |
ISBN 9798765106778 (pdf) Subjects: LCSH: Modest Mouse (Musical group).
Moon & Antarctica. | Alternative rock music–United States–History and criticism. |
Rock music–1991-2000–United States–History and criticism.
Classification: LCC ML421.M62 P47 2024 (print) | LCC ML421.M62 (ebook) |
DDC 782.42166092/2–dc23/eng/20240501
LC record available at https://lccn.loc.gov/2024019622
LC ebook record available at https://lccn.loc.gov/2024019623

ISBN: PB: 979-8-7651-0675-4
ePDF: 979-8-7651-0677-8
eBook: 979-8-7651-0676-1

Series: 33 1/3

Typeset by Deanta Global Publishing Services, Chennai, India
Printed and bound in the United States

To find out more about our authors and books visit www.bloomsbury.com
and sign up for our newsletters.

For Geoff.

*With gratitude to everyone who mined their minds
for this book.*

*And with apologies at large for the 100 variations of the word
"fuck" that appear throughout it (er, 101).*

This book is a work of nonfiction. But it is also a work of an unreliable narrator: memory.

And as he would probably agree: Isaac Brock.

"Recently, I've been writing a lot of songs about the devil and outer space. I'm not really into God or any of that shit, but I'm pretty sure I got a visit from the devil."
—Isaac Brock, *The Reader*, October 15, 1998

Contents

By Way of Introduction: Fuck You, Cowboy   1

Welcome to Ice Cream Party   7

Building Nothing Out of Something   11

The Devil's Apprentice   23

Emptying the Bottle   29

Blending Burgers   43

Aside: *Everywhere and His Nasty Parlour Tricks*   51

The Moon & Antarctica   59
   "3rd Planet"   68
   "Gravity Rides Everything"   73
   "Dark Center of the Universe"   76
   "Perfect Disguise"   76
   "Tiny Cities Made of Ashes"   80
   "A Different City"   83
   "The Cold Part"   84
   "Alone Down There"   85
   "The Stars Are Projectors"   88
   "Wild Packs of Family Dogs"   92
   "Paper Thin Walls"   93
   "I Came as a Rat"   95

CONTENTS

"Lives" 97

"Life Like Weeds" 99

"What People Are Made Of" 102

Aside: Jeremiah Green 107

VI · XIII · MM 117

Aftermath 125

Coda 131

Appendix 135

Bibliography 138

Acknowledgments 143

By Way of Introduction
Fuck You, Cowboy

It was a terrible idea from the start.

But to be fair, Isaac Brock has always commanded a certain degree of chaos—on stage, in interviews, and all places beyond. A seasoned Modest Mouse concertgoer knows not to set expectations for any given live show but rather to wholly jettison them. As the years have gone by, you just never know which Brock will take the stage: the subdued and seemingly pensive Brock; the cryptically buzzed Brock prone to droll turns of phrase; the Brock screaming into his pickups, so possessed by the jagged riffs and haunting harmonics that for the briefest of moments, you believe you have caught a glimpse of the raw materials of Modest Mouse's creative output.

Of course, chaos goes both ways.

It was 1999, and songwriter/guitarist Isaac Brock, drummer Jeremiah Green, and bassist Eric Judy were in Chicago.

That night, Brock and friends had emptied various bottles at the bar/venue the Empty Bottle and headed back to Modest Mouse's fledgling apartment above the nascent Clava Studios in the Bridgeport neighborhood of Chicago. In Brock's account, he wanted a cigarette. So he fired one up—and he decided to walk across the street to Armour

Square Park, near the White Sox stadium, to "shoot the shit" with a dozen-plus people gathered there.

"Then the 'fuck you cowboy' event happened," Brock says.

He recalls moseying up to the group and offering a salutation: "How y'all doing?"

No one turned. Someone shrugged. And then, out of the corner of his eye, he saw the fist coming.

"It just happened," he says. "I was just like a golf ball on a tee."

Brock drunkenly explored his face with one hand and turned to his assailant. "You broke my jaw!" he marveled.

He remembers walking slowly away, bottles whizzing past his head. Others present that night remember him running, fleeing in a Western shirt with a dog named Spooky.

"Fuck you, cowboy!" someone called into the night after him.

All of this would likely have been a footnoted anecdote in those early bedlam days of Isaac Brock—were it not for what the band was in Chicago to do: record their major-label debut.

It was producer Brian Deck's first major-label project.

It was the first album to be recorded in Deck's new studio, Clava . . . where Brock's friends were helping to hang drywall and finish construction as he worked to finish the songs.

It was the most ambitious creative endeavor Modest Mouse had ever embarked upon.

And now, with just one day of vocals recorded, Brock emerged from a hospital with his jaw completely wired shut.

How all this was going to work was anyone's guess.

* * *

In October 1999, attendees of the first Coachella music festival were likely particularly unprepared for *The Moon & Antarctica*. Having materialized from the haze of the studio, where he'd been obsessively layering sounds on the record, Brock famously decided he'd had enough of his jaw being wired shut. He was self-conscious and felt he probably looked angry while singing with his mouth clenched, so—

"I unwired it with a Leatherman and some booze in a hotel room," he says matter-of-factly. "I had no idea how much it was actually going to hurt. I did such a bad job."

In turn, he downed some of his pain meds, and, well—

"I don't know if we even finished a fucking song," he says of the Coachella performance.

It's a testament to the at times bipolar nature of Modest Mouse that the band wrapped up recording the next month and released the highly polished *Moon & Antarctica* in June 2000.

As Brent DiCrescenzo—a *Pitchfork* author who excelled at critical gelding, if not wholesale evisceration—wrote on the site in a 9.8/10 review:

Every so often—whether due to astronomical occurrences, economic fluctuations, or inherent quality cycles (which have all actually been debated at one point)—an album comes along that inhibits our serotonin uptake, cleans our ears, palpitates our hearts, ignites our passion, and justifies our existence. I've argued that this occurs approximately every three years, due to slight financial recessions. It's that time again. At this point, I think the world agrees on *OK Computer* as the last major event in album rock. For at least a few months, the world can stop waiting for Radiohead's next album, and start wondering how in the hell Modest Mouse will ever top the monumental, groundbreaking, hypnotic, sublime *The Moon & Antarctica*.

The band's raw production of yesteryear and flirtations with the experimental gave way to shining highs, roving epics like "The Stars Are Projectors," and an all-around cosmic, nuanced concept album that left the listener wondering, like the aforementioned *OK Computer* before it, exactly where the hell all this came from in the first place.

NME has since dubbed it "hands-down one of the greatest records ever made."

Moreover, as Steven Hyden wrote on *Uproxx* on the album's twentieth anniversary in 2020,

> *The Moon & Antarctica* is a crucial pivot point not just for the band but for indie music overall. If Modest Mouse's early albums helped to define the boilerplate sound of '90s indie rock—chunky guitars, a loose and bombastic rhythm section, shout-y vocals, wry and often insightful lyrics—*The Moon & Antarctica* paved the way for what indie became in the 21st century.

And yet after appearing on the Billboard 200 chart for two weeks and peaking at No. 120 . . . *The Moon & Antarctica* fell off.

"What I think I did is made a very hard record for Epic to sell or market," Brock says. "Not nearly as hard as I thought I was going to, though."

Ironically, Modest Mouse's major-label debut would be their most experimental. Simultaneously, as Hyden and others have detailed, it helped to dispel the notion of a band "selling out" by releasing work on a corporate label or licensing music for commercial endeavors.

In further irony—and likely to Epic's joy—the sprawling arrangements of *The Moon & Antarctica* eventually yielded simpler songs, which culminated in the hit follow-up *Good News for People Who Love Bad News* and its endlessly cycled single "Float On" ("everyone and their frat brother fuckin' like that record," Brock notes).

Ultimately, *The Moon & Antarctica* is an album so strange and enigmatic, from those sweet opening notes, to the plunging depths of the middle, to the shocking, furious end, that you almost hesitate to listen to it again for fear of it losing its luster. But then you do, and you discover all new sounds—a lost harmonic here, a stray percussion element there, a fresh interpretation of a lyric that leaves you thunderstruck.

And that ever-looming question, two-and-a-half decades on: *How the fuck did Modest Mouse pull this off?*

Welcome to Ice Cream Party

I feel bad for the hypnotist.

After entering Ice Cream Party—Modest Mouse's home base, gear repository, and recording studio in Portland's Goose Hollow neighborhood, which shares its name with a 2019 song by the band—she proceeds past Isaac Brock's voluminous gem collection in the entry room. Then, it's on to the cathedral of oddity in the soaring light- and plant- and instrument- and tschotske-filled main atrium. Beneath the gaze of taxidermied birds and Victorian-garmented rabbit dolls, we head past one of those coin-operated grocery store ponies to the basement stairwell. Sandwiched between a writer wielding a voice recorder and a guy wearing a shirt covered in psychedelic mushrooms and tattoos ranging from a pitchfork to assorted flora and fauna, she seems to be taking the general weirdness of the assignment in stride.

Brock navigates through a dark corridor of amplifiers to our destination, the studio control room where Modest Mouse's sixth album, *Strangers to Ourselves*, was recorded. He steps out for a moment, and I attempt to explain our predicament to the hypnotist: he's a musician, and I'm writing a book about how one of his albums got made.

But there's a problem. And it's perhaps a critical, damning, all-encompassing one: he doesn't remember much about writing or recording it. It could be the Vicodin and the jaw. It could be the twenty-five years in the interim. But he doesn't remember. So his camp reached out to you to see if you could help him with some recall work.

Brock returns and is directed to lie down on the couch, where he admits that he has seen nine (!) different hypnotists to help him quit smoking cigarettes . . . to no avail. She begins attempting to put him under.

"Our mind is capable of recording everything," she says, drawing a parallel between the hypnosis at hand and his livelihood. "What do you do with your recordings? How do you store them?"

"On a hard drive."

"How do you find the things that you want to find in that hard drive?"

"Well," he says, "I usually type in the name that I remember. But oftentimes, I gave it some stupid name that I thought I'd remember. And I don't remember. And I end up having to call four different people and ask them if they remember anything about the file. And that's how an hour goes by. It's actually not far from how my real memory works. Which is to say, it's not very organized."

She tries a few more strategies. Eventually, it all yields just a single memory from the era: driving across the country from Seattle to Chicago with multi-instrumentalist Ben Blankenship, who would play on some of the tracks on *The Moon & Antarctica*.

"He kept claiming to have eaten brains on tacos once in Missoula, Montana. And so I took him to the restaurant . . . kind of being an asshole to prove that he hadn't done it. And I ordered him brain tacos. And he took one bite, and he looked sick."

She maintains composure; I desperately try not to laugh and derail the whole thing.

"For some reason it was important to him to have once eaten them. And then it was important to me to call bullshit on it. Well, it wasn't important. It was petty."

She tries another tactic: given that Brock's hands were intimately involved in crafting the record, she suggests he pick up one of the many guitars in the room to see what muscle memory might elicit. He gives it a go and plucks the opening notes of "3rd Planet," the first track on *The Moon & Antarctica* . . . but the guitar is out of tune. He bemoans that he just paid someone to tune all the instruments down here while he was out on tour and then sits—but doesn't lay—down.

"I don't know if I'm having much luck with the recall right now," he says with a sigh, eyes open. "I feel like this might be a waste of everyone's time, if that's fair. I don't feel like I'm being able to really get in there in the way I wanted. . . . I'm sorry. I hope that's not offensive."

She tells him that's absolutely fine, but offers to try talking a bit more.

"Recently, I had a friend pass away," Brock says. "He was part of the band." Brock is referring to founding Modest Mouse drummer Jeremiah Green, who died from cancer at age forty-five just a few months earlier. "He was part of these recordings. I realized before he passed away that he remembers a lot of shit I don't. And I remember shit he doesn't. And that we collectively, as a group, all retain different parts of the story. And when one of us disappears, a percentage of the story and the details is gone. . . . I think my best bet is to do [the interviews for the book] the way I always do—which is to ramble and drink."

Earlier, the hypnotist had said she always wanted to learn a musical instrument. Brock now asks her which instrument she wants to learn. She says ukulele. He offers to have her come over and play with him and his neighbor, who's an excellent ukulele player. They trade info.

Then we head out the back door of the studio and down the alley to pick up some canned Modelo Cheladas.

He has decided to do it the hard way.

Building Nothing Out of Something

When *This Is a Long Drive for Someone with Nothing to Think About* formally kicked off Modest Mouse's career in 1996, listeners were presented with a startling variety of sonic geography, from the desolate, reverb-rich soundscapes of "Dramamine" and "Ohio" to the utter madness of "Tundra/ Desert" and "Make Everyone Happy/Mechanical Birds." Every track surprised—and the album collectively gave listeners an insight into the scale of possibility of the band.

A year later, *The Lonesome Crowded West* tightened everything all at once, providing a more cohesive collection while introducing a rich cast of characters and a conceptual throughline, cementing Modest Mouse as local heroes in post-grunge Seattle, and drawing the attention of major labels (more on that in a moment).

Much has been written about the lore surrounding Isaac Brock's upbringing—and I encourage you to dig around on it, by virtue of the fact that there's just too much of it to delve into here, especially when it comes to parsing fact from fiction. For our purposes, Brock largely grew up in Issaquah, Washington, a town of 40,000 or so, the son of a free-spirited mother who left Brock's father for Brock's uncle.

(Modest Mouse mythology often frames her as a radical member of the White Panther Party who raised Brock in a hippie commune and/or Branch Davidian cult, but that's all largely embellished.) Brock says he started writing songs when he was fourteen or fifteen, soon meeting bassist Eric Judy in a video store. At the time, Brock also played bass . . . and thus Modest Mouse was originally just two basses before everything coalesced with the addition of Green. After a flood at his mother's house, Brock temporarily set up shop in a shed on the family's property—and that's where Modest Mouse truly began.

The music the three would go on to create together has engendered a fair amount of comparisons over the years—with copious Built to Spill citations—but the most resonant are the Pixies nods. Yes, there's the screams and snarls, the forays into the off-kilter, the chaotic moments, the blissful and tender sweet spots—but to me, it's the fact that when one first listens to the Pixies, they're utterly confused by virtue of having never heard anything like it before. (Remember the first time you put on *Surfer Rosa* and "Bone Machine" started playing?) The same goes for Modest Mouse. Whether your starting point was the quasi-terrifying "Dirty Fingernails" or "Never Ending Math Equation" (the latter of which previews the balance of the personal and cosmic that would go on to define *The Moon & Antarctica*), there's a good chance you were left feeling like you had heard something truly new. Brock says that was the goal.

"I was, and still am, pretty fucking determined to try and find shit that doesn't sound canned. And that's tricky, so it starts getting more and more herky-jerky," he says from a table in the center of Ice Cream Party that serves as a gathering place and central nervous system. Also, "I wasn't very good. So writing strange was a pretty good workaround to [not] being technically skilled."

Brock's longtime friend and former Modest Mouse tour manager Sean Hurley says that in the lead up to *The Moon & Antarctica*, he remembers the band being very into the blues-infused indie outfit Red Red Meat and the rolling arrangements of the German experimental rock band CAN—which one can indeed feel on the album. (A good exercise: listen to "Tiny Cities Made of Ashes" alongside CAN's "Vitamin C.") Hurley, who lived with Brock in that era, also remembers hearing bits and pieces of "3rd Planet" around the house, though he says Brock tended to keep his artistic vision close to his chest.

Ultimately, *The Moon & Antarctica* is a record very *not* of its time. In the mid- to late-1990s, indie and punk fans cared deeply about a deeply irrelevant thing, at least by today's standards: "Selling out." To do anything commercial—or, God forbid, sign with a major label—was artistic heresy. As a teenager in the era, I recall having discussions about the ethics of different bands and labels that bordered on the theological, often over dinner at assorted chain restaurants or to the tune of CDs we had purchased at big-box stores.

Brock's line of thinking at the time? He wanted a bigger recording budget. He wanted *The Moon & Antarctica*, which would turn the lens of the music from his fixation on the creeping corporate decay of the Pacific Northwest to the universe beyond, to be something more than the sum of the band's first two records.

"I was feeling ambitious," he put it to me with a shrug in one early conversation.

Brock offered more insight to the Chicago alt-weekly *The Reader* in 1998: "I have a limited education. I don't want to be working shit jobs my whole life without the possibility of having a chance to even own my own house. I wouldn't mind actually getting paid. . . Commercial rock is usually pretty shitty, but it doesn't have to stay that way."

As straightforward as it all sounds today, for the indie scene at the turn of the millennium, it was akin to an act of treason in the eyes of fans and, of course, music journalists. When it came to signing with a major label, "I was having a really hard time coming to terms with that," Brock says. "And so I wanted to make sure I didn't make an easy record or a pop record."

Whereas Brock has forgotten swaths of the creation of *The Moon & Antarctica*, others remember. Well, bits and pieces, anyway. But collectively, they form a mosaic.

Matt Marshall is a career A&R rep who today is with Fantasy Recordings. In the late 1990s, he was with Sony and had fallen in love with *The Lonesome Crowded West*. He was interested in signing the band to the Sony subsidiary Epic Records. And if fans had anxiety about Modest Mouse signing to a major label, well, Marshall was right there with them.

"Listen, one of my goals was to not mess up a band that I loved," he says. "I've seen too many examples of great indie bands signing to a major and feeling like they had to make a 'major label record' and the A&R person there forcing them to use some big commercial producer. And the results, with few exceptions—and there are exceptions—were disastrous. My whole thing was, I fell in love with Modest Mouse—I want them to keep doing exactly what they're doing."

Marshall and the band began feeling each other out, a process he says would occupy the better part of a year. Brock recalls asking Marshall what would happen if, say, the band turned in a wholly experimental record that was the antithesis of a commercial release, and he remembers Marshall saying that they would indeed put it out; they just wouldn't put a lot of money into it. (Remember that for later.)

Brock tested the waters with Marshall by sharing rather profound proof of concept for what he was looking to create—the early 1999 Phil Ek–recorded demos that would go on to largely become the original *Night on the Sun* EP and also inform the *Everywhere and His Nasty Parlour Tricks* EP: "Night on the Sun," "You're the Good Things (It's Alright to Die)," "Wild Packs of Family Dogs," "Dark Center of the Universe," and "You're Life," which would later become "Lives."[1]

---

[1] This track listing would appear on the first *Night on the Sun* EP, released in CD form by Japanese label Rebel Beat Factory. The 700 copies were exclusively sold during Modest Mouse's 1999 summer tour of Japan, and the EP features a final track where Jeremiah Green thanks listeners, in Japanese, for purchasing it. (Whether "You're Life" was some Brockian wordplay or a misprint on the back of the CD, I do not know.) This isn't to be confused with the US/UK vinyl edition of *Night on the Sun*, produced and recorded by Brian Deck and released by Up Records a year later, featuring "Willful Suspension of Disbelief," "Night on the Sun," "I Came as a Rat (Long Walk Off a Short Dock)," and "You're the Good Things."

"These were the first five that were written for [*The Moon & Antarctica*]," Brock says as he lights a cigarette from his perch at Ice Cream Party, the smoking having moved indoors to match pace with the drinking. "I wasn't holding anything back."

With a bevy of songs that would go on to become Modest Mouse classics, Brock's cards were on the table. The band was talking to other labels, but in the end, they shook hands with Matt Marshall.

"My speech on integrity went like this," Brock says. "If I'm doing something I enjoy and I'm making money and things and I use my art to make money . . . don't question my integrity, because where's my integrity when I'm washing dishes for minimum wage or selling fucking plasma or whatever?"

Following the signing, Marshall says two types of people kept coming up to him at Epic. "Half the people were sort of mean about it, saying, 'What are you doing signing a band like Modest Mouse? They have no place on a major label. What are you thinking? They'll never sell more than 200,000 records.' And then I had people who were really nice and came up to me and said, 'Oh my god, I love that band, what a great signing. I so love Modest Mouse . . . but I hope you realize they'll never sell more than 200,000 records.'"

It was a small deal by major label standards (Brock says the band netted an $85,000 recording budget, which was an insane amount of money to him).[2] Had the band broken a

[2]Recollections around how much the deal was for are a bit scattered by source. Perhaps the truth lies in the past—Eric Judy told a newspaper in

few years earlier when record execs were mining everything in Seattle to death, Marshall says a bidding war would have ensued. But small though the deal may have been, it came with concessions on behalf of the label: namely, that Modest Mouse's former indie home of Up Records could release the (ultimately beloved) A- and B-side compilation *Building Nothing Out of Something*, and that Brock could release his Ugly Casanova side project, which he did through Sub Pop.

And there was perhaps one more allowance: a largely untested producer named Brian Deck.

*   *   *

Red Red Meat percussionist—and current Modest Mouse member—Ben Massarella recalls the first time he saw Brock, Green, and Judy on stage. The various members of Red Red Meat had been scattered about the venue, but after Modest Mouse started playing, they all began to magnetically coalesce in front of the stage.

"There was hardly anybody else in the place, and we were just like, 'These guys are gonna be fucking huge. They're for real,'" Massarella marvels. "It was awesome."

Brian Deck says he first met Brock when Modest Mouse opened for Red Red Meat in Chicago. Deck was Red Red Meat's drummer, in addition to mixing and engineering such recordings as the band's final album, *There's a Star Above the*

2000 that Modest Mouse had gotten $100,000 for the record, "a substantial boost from the $10,000 to $15,000 budgets the band was used to working with."

Manger Tonight (which *Pitchfork* would later declare "the place where Red Red Meat fully discovered the studio-as-instrument").

Music was played. Many beers were consumed.

"They were so young," Deck recalls from his Chicago recording studio, Narwhal. "They were just so full of excitement and energy all the time, and it was a little overwhelming, but it was so impressive to see them harness that on stage. Obviously, Isaac was just a brilliant stream-of-consciousness improviser of everything—conversation, behavior, as well as music."

Time passed. *The Lonesome Crowded West* was released. Red Red Meat fell apart, and a few of the band's members would continue to collaborate as Califone, originally Tim Rutili's solo project. But this time around, Deck says, Califone opened for Modest Mouse.

At some point, Brock says Rutili had asked him to join the band. So Brock drove across the country to Chicago, where Califone was based, paying the owner of the Empty Bottle one dollar a month to sleep on the floor of the bar's unfinished upper level. He went to his first practice with Califone, which was held at the art deco truck wash Massarella had inherited from his father . . . and discovered that everyone was playing in open guitar tunings. Problem was, Brock didn't know any alternate tunings. And thus it was a disaster.

"I'm just self-taught, and not self-taught that well," he says. "I basically just ate shit. Like, there's no reason I would have kept me in the band. I got one fucking practice, and then I was given a job cleaning up meat trucks at

[Massarella's] truck stop—which was super fun because you got to work drunk."

Dismissed from the band, Brock bided his time spraying blood out of said meat trucks (as he described it to one interviewer in 1998: "The most fun job I've had in a while. Livers and shit on the floor, huge big chunks of fat the size of your head that are all kind of hard like butter").

But he did get one thing out of the whole ordeal that would shape Modest Mouse's future output: he asked Rutili what his favorite open tuning was. And he left Chicago with the open E he would use to write tracks like "Night on the Sun" and "A Different City."

Somewhere along the line, Brock says he deduced that Deck had done a lot of the recording and producing for Red Red Meat and Califone—so he proposed his name to Marshall for *The Moon & Antarctica*. Marshall then flew to Chicago to meet Deck and give him a once-over, and says he loved him. But ultimately, you get the sense that it wouldn't have really mattered if he hadn't.

"At that point, Modest Mouse had made a number of records without me," Marshall says. "My whole thing was, I'm not going to mess with them. I want to be prepared if it's not working, but [my goal was to] let them make a Modest Mouse record. I was not trying to turn them into anything else."

All Deck knew of Marshall was that he had been the person who'd originally signed Tool. And that indicated to him that he was open-minded and progressive. Yet still, he was nervous. Or, rather—

"I was fucking terrified. It was absolutely the first exposure I'd had personally to doing anything for a major label. And I had impostor syndrome. Enormously."

But he had his studio . . . at least for a brief moment. Deck and Massarella had created a recording studio dubbed Clava, a portmanteau of the names of each of their daughters, Clara and Ava. They had rented the top-floor ballroom of a four-story walk-up in Pilsen, complete with twelve-foot ceilings, heavy plaster walls, and thick oak floors—a great hub for recording. Boasting a variety of rooms with distinct sounds, he says Brock was excited to work there. But then Clava got kicked out.

If you've ever been to Pilsen on Chicago's Lower West Side, it's an area defined by its brilliant Mexican culture. Residents displaced by the construction of the University of Illinois at Chicago had relocated to the neighborhood in large numbers in the early 1960s and had since been organized in fiercely rejecting gentrification efforts. And, well, "rightly so," Deck says. "They should have kicked us out because we were total first-wave gentrifiers. The guy that we were renting from was open to renting to us, but the Chamber of Commerce got to him and said, 'You've got to kick these guys out.'"

It probably didn't help Deck's impostor syndrome that now, with Modest Mouse soon to travel to Chicago to record their major-label debut, the producer no longer had a studio. And so Deck and friends rushed to find a new location, which they did in Bridgeport. They set up shop in a residential neighborhood directly across from Comiskey Park, anchoring the studio in a converted garage, utilizing the rest of the space as an office for Massarella and Rutili's label Perishable Records, and reserving the apartment upstairs to host bands.

Deck says Massarella was funding the whole thing with money earned from liquidating the truck wash assets he had inherited—and cash was running low. So Deck called Marshall.

"I was kind of in nervous breakdown mode," Deck says. "I was afraid that when I made that phone call, he would laugh at me and say, 'No, you know what? I'm tired of fucking around with clowns. We're gonna go have this done by a real engineer at a studio that exists.'"

Instead, Deck says Marshall advanced them half the budget for the record so they could buy the rest of the necessary equipment, notably a compressor.

Now, if you read virtually anything about the making of *The Moon & Antarctica*, you're going to come across three well-worn stories: the story of Brock getting his jaw broken, the story of him unwiring it himself . . . and the story of how, when Modest Mouse arrived at Clava following Ben Blankenship's tacos de sesos—the aforementioned brains—they arrived to a studio that was only half-built. And that's true. But not entirely the truth.

As it turns out, the band showed up more than a week early.

Deck says he tried to hold them off as they kept sending pings from across the country, drawing closer and closer. "They kept calling me every day, being like . . . 'we're on our way.' I'm like, 'Please just go to the Badlands and camp for a week. We're not ready.'" Camp, they did not. And so when they arrived, Judy, Green, and Hurley, the last of whom had joined the band on its cross-country trek, found themselves helping to hang drywall.

"It was fucking chaos," says Hurley. "There became a little bit of a vibe among Modest Mouse—like, are these guys fucking us over?"

For his part, Brock says he remembers helping a little bit, but he had another job: finishing the songs, which also weren't all the way done. However, "I wasn't too stressed. I didn't have anything else going on."

Judy says he wasn't all that worried either. He does recall, however, one specific thing about arriving in Chicago.

"When we got there we did a little tarot reading, and it was all this doomsday and terrible stuff," he says.

From a home in the Chicago suburbs today, Greg Ratajczak, Clava's intern and subsequent assistant at the time, fondly remembers insulation wrapped in fabric and all the other details of the rushed, half-assed construction job.

"It was as crude as crude can be. But that was the charm of it. And Brian did a magnificent job. I mean, it was a great-sounding room. You hear it on the fucking record, you hear it all over that fucking record."

As part of his gig, Ratajczak got free room and board above the studio in the 750-ish square foot apartment . . . with his new roommates, Eric Judy, Jeremiah Green, and Isaac Brock. He says he immediately hit it off with Green and Judy. Brock, however, was a different story.

"Isaac came with a bit of a, *Hey—watch out*. He came with a warning," Ratajczak says. "Not [that he's] a bad guy, but *be aware this guy is kind of an interesting character* . . . "

The Devil's Apprentice

Modest Mouse is often heralded for Isaac Brock's poignant reflections on blue-collar life, but what has always seemed remarkable to me is the way those themes and the myriad beyond are framed from a literary standpoint. As a book nerd myself, I recognize the book nerd in Brock (and, for that matter, Eric Judy, who now owns and operates Paper Boat Booksellers in Seattle). The output of Modest Mouse has long resonated with other book nerds I know, and for good reason, starting with the band's name itself: "modest mouse" is lifted from a passage in Virginia Woolf's 1917 short story "The Mark on the Wall," which reads:

> I wish I could hit upon a pleasant track of thought, a track indirectly reflecting credit upon myself, for those are the pleasantest thoughts, and very frequent even in the minds of modest mouse-coloured people, who believe genuinely that they dislike to hear their own praises. They are not thoughts directly praising oneself; that is the beauty of them.

Rather than subject you to literary criticism about the passage, what most strikes me is how Woolf's signature stream-of-consciousness flow is not wholly dissimilar from having a chat with Brock. A conversation about quitting smoking organically evolves into a story about trying to intimidate an intruder on his property by wielding a BB gun in the wee hours of the night; a tour of some of the bookshelves at Ice Cream Party, boasting curiosities like the upper management manuals for Scientology, eventually gives way to discussion of the time "I lost my mind and bought a lot of stained glass" and the time "I tried losing all my money in a bar," that being the short-lived Portland watering hole Poison's Rainbow, which Brock co-owned.

It's not awkward or disjointed. It just is. Dialogue tends to develop like a chrysalis in fast forward, quickly evolving to curious maturation and taking flight before you have a chance to fully seize upon it and inspect it. And then onto the next moth. (As for all those "fucks" and "shits," you eventually stop hearing the swears that punctuate Brock's language the way "um" or "like" might another's vernacular— while amping up your own curse words, either to keep pace or because somehow a tacit agreement has been made that there's no point in pretending that verboten yet benign words don't belong in the course of everyday conversation.)

Elsewhere, there are other overt literary references throughout Modest Mouse's output—such as Brock's banjo-driven take on Charles Bukowski from *Good News for People Who Love Bad News* that's equal parts hilarious and reflective. ("God, who'd want to be such an asshole?") To that end, when it comes to the appraisal of Modest Mouse's work, perhaps more than anything, critics and fans celebrate Brock's wordplay. It can be blunt and hilarious, like in "Bukowski," but more often than not on *The Moon & Antarctica* it's powerfully enigmatic.

You were the dull sound of sharp math when you were alive. Where does it all come from?

As a kid, Brock read a lot (er, "a shit-ton") and loved C. S. Lewis' *The Chronicles of Narnia*. When he was eleven, he got a job running spotlights in a theater before progressing to the light board and sound duties. Between cues, he read voraciously—everything Vonnegut had ever written, *The Lord of the Rings*, books about social or environmental politics, *The Anarchist Cookbook*.[1]

"[Six or] seven days a fucking week I was in this box working at a theater," he says. "I read so much I missed cues and would get in trouble. People would start singing their part and the lights wouldn't come on."

Around the time of *The Moon & Antarctica*, Brock had just finished reading Cormac McCarthy's dark, violent, and visceral *Blood Meridian*. "And that had a huge, huge and lasting impact on me."

Indeed, following the release of the album, Brock told MTV that he wanted to create an album that sounded like a Cormac McCarthy book—"I wanted to make a really dark landscape, musically and lyrically." To that end, he says

---

[1]"I remember getting *The Anarchist Cookbook* and thinking that was pretty cool, but then being like, *Oh, this is actually maybe a little shittier than I want to be as a person.*"

the overall vibe he was seeking to capture came from an experience he had prior to the album.[2]

"I'm not sure how crazy I want to sound yet."

Go on.

"But there's a waking nightmare that I had. It was like someone was standing on my chest and I couldn't fucking move or anything. I'm not a religious person; [I was] stone-cold sober. Something other than me was there. And it was spooky and it kind of prompted a bit of this shit. I'm not a dude of the scriptures, but I think there's a lot of shit out there that we can't see. In dark matter alone, we could be coexisting with shit that we just literally can't see, and they can't see us. Our atoms are fucking vibrating in just the right fucking way that we're literally invisible and walking through each other all the time."

He later added that the experience was how others would describe a demonic possession.

"It shook me, man. There's something about that feeling I just kept wanting to write about. I felt like I was taken over. The whole event only lasted maybe thirty seconds, but there's like a cold and fucking unreasonable terror . . . like something passed through and left some pretty good boot marks on me."

---

[2]Worth noting here: Brock and the band openly toyed with journalists early in their career. He is an unreliable narrator by his own admission, warning me up front that his recollections could vary by the day—but he consistently told me the following story on two different occasions separated by more than a year.

Brock fidgets with a massive bowie knife atop a calendar in front of him.

"It's a lot to imagine or take in, but I find it kind of comforting to know that we might not just be against the wall of reality . . . because we're doing really bad at it."

Perhaps unsurprisingly, this is a subject we'll be circling back to when we discuss the song "Alone Down There."

Another influence on *The Moon & Antarctica*: C. S. Lewis' Space Trilogy—*Out of the Silent Planet*, *Perelandra*, and *That Hideous Strength*—which was originally published between 1938 and 1945. Brock says he read them initially in high school and also probably reread them around the time of recording the album. The trilogy largely documents the journeys of philologist Elwin Ransom, featuring an exiled Earth, nefarious technocrats, a cosmic battle of good and evil, and even demonic possession.

He doesn't remember specifically how it all shows up in the album—again, much has been forgotten, he reminds me, and I remind you—just that it does, with one caveat:

"I don't want to make it sound like I read two books and fucking tried to make a record about those books. That's not what happened. But if there was anything where I was trying to get a vibe that wasn't coming from inside me, it would be that."

He cracks another Chelada.

Emptying the Bottle

Given the dearth of collective memory around the earliest recording sessions for *The Moon & Antarctica*, perhaps the most accurate way to write this chapter would be a two-word summation: *They happened.*

Of any part of the process, this stage seems to be the most nebulous in memory. But to pull a bit of thread, let's start with some tech specs: Brian Deck says he used a 3M M79 two-inch sixteen-track tape machine to capture the basic elements that form the foundation of the record. Drums and bass were recorded to tape and mixed from tape, and a couple of the early guitars were recorded to tape and used as well.

Clava's young assistant at the time, Greg Ratajczak, says most of the bass was captured on his Ampeg B-15, and the group used everything they had for guitars—a Fender Twin, Deck's Magnatone for clean guitars, maybe an Orange Pics Only or 120 Ratajczak was borrowing.

As for the studio itself, that converted garage was a tight space. Deck doesn't have any photos of Clava from when Modest Mouse recorded the album, but he does have photos of Iron & Wine (for whom he would produce *Our Endless Numbered Days* and other releases) rehearsing for a tour there. The walls appear to be a light green hue; there's a control room and requisite window; an isolation booth that was home to guitar amps; a booth and window where bass was typically recorded. Deck also points out that the space had a low ceiling—just over seven feet high in the middle and lower on the sides. Ultimately, it made for an organically great sound.

When it came to the song compositions for what became *The Moon & Antarctica*, Eric Judy says the band adhered to their usual process at the time—sometimes Isaac Brock would come in with a song, and he and Jeremiah Green would build it out with their parts. Or, the band would find the songs through jamming and flesh things out that way— or wholly invent them in the studio, which is how he believes "Tiny Cities Made of Ashes" came to be. ("Jeremy and Eric's contribution is so fucking obvious," Brock says. "If I had two different people in the room rather than them it wouldn't have been the same record.")

As for the basic tracking, Brock doesn't intellectualize it and says it's not a creative exercise—you play the songs until you get a good take. The creative act has already happened elsewhere, and the job is now to get it down on tape.

In the build-up to *The Moon & Antarctica*, Sean Hurley remembers the band's live shows evolving (or devolving, if you're the type of person who wants to hear a live track exactly as it was recorded) into often-sprawling experimental jams.[1] And when it came to how the group wanted to

---

[1] Some of these shows can be found on YouTube in full. An early favorite of mine: the band playing the laundromat/venue Sudsy Malone's in Cincinnati

capture everything in studio, per Deck, "I definitely remember talking about how they explore a song live, and how much improvisation there is, and open-endedness to the arrangements—and wanting to incorporate that into the recording process, and not necessarily make tightly constructed pop songs. And there are some tightly constructed pop songs. But then there's 'Stars Are Projectors.'"

The degree to which producers involve themselves in such things as song compositions varies wildly (often to incredible success, it should be noted). Looking back on the record today, Brock says Deck didn't really meddle deeply with structures or anything like that—he just captured the overall vibe.

While those sessions are also hazy in Deck's mind today, he offered this to *Electronic Musician* in January 2001:

> Instead of being specific sometimes about an overdub idea, I'd suggest to the band, "This idea is too organized. You need to go choose an instrument you've never played before and come up with something right away." Or, "This is really even. Think about prime numbers and go try this again." You know, just ridiculous things, "oblique strategies" and other Brian Eno-type things to say to them to trigger a different way of thinking.
>
> There are a lot of different variations and mind games that you can play on yourself and other people in the studio, just to grease the wheels; even if nothing comes

in November 1997, which includes an insane, ten-minute-plus rendition of "Dirty Fingernails" and a lengthy early version of "Lives."

---

of it directly, it can be that mental colonic that people need.

Another mental colonic the band perhaps needed: the casting out of Ben Blankenship, the guy Brock says he forced to eat those brain tacos en route to Chicago. In the interviews conducted for this book, Blankenship was either almost absent from the conversations around the record, or no one really seemed to know what to say when I brought him up. Per the album's liner notes, he played lap steel on "3rd Planet," banjo and lap steel on "Perfect Disguise," keyboards on "Tiny Cities Made of Ashes," "Paper Thin Walls," and "Life Like Weeds," and guitar on "Alone Down There," "Paper Thin Walls," and "What People Are Made Of."

He undoubtedly made a contribution to the record. So, what gives?

"Ben Blankenship was a problem," Deck says. According to the producer, Blankenship had done some touring with the band, and Brock wanted a bit of outside influence on the music; problem was, he quickly got on the band's nerves. So Deck removed him from the basic tracking process to keep the sanctity and balance of the core trio—and ultimately, he says he and Brock decided Blankenship was a toxic presence, "possibly by no fault of his own." After basic tracking was complete, Deck says they let him have a run at everything and then sent him on his way.

The one contribution everyone does indeed remember, and in a glowing light, is Blankenship's guitar work on "Paper Thin Walls," which we'll discuss soon enough.

Another not entirely welcome presence in the studio: A&R rep Matt Marshall. At least at first.

"I didn't want him to come because I was certain he would realize that I was fucking this up and shouldn't be in charge of this," says Deck—a man who, it's worth noting, projects confidence and wisdom to an almost intimidating degree. "He demonstrated his trust in ways that he didn't have to. That was extremely appreciated and made the whole thing much better, and it blew me away. By the end of the situation, he was a best friend and a mentor, and he did things for me in the business that he didn't need to have done."

Marshall says his goal in studios has always been to never overstay his welcome. For *The Moon & Antarctica*, he recalls dropping by for a couple days just to make sure all was well.

"I sat there watching, just enjoying the hell out of myself because I was watching these amazing songs come to life," he says. "And after two or three days, Isaac said to me, 'Aren't you going to give us your opinions on the music?' And I said, 'Well, until now you haven't asked me.' . . . In my mind that was [an important] thing, because [they could have figured], *Oh, the major label guy is going to come in and try to fuck with us.* And when I said that, he said, 'I always want to know your opinion—please share it on anything.' And I think it just set up a much better relationship, which we've maintained for twenty years now. I think secure artists who really are confident in what they do don't mind opinions."

Soon enough, the tracking was done. Everyone had declared it finished, and Judy and Green headed home.

According to Deck, Brock had just concluded his first day of real vocals.

"We were so happy," Deck says. "It was going so well; we all felt so great."

That night, Deck went home. And Brock, his girlfriend, and Hurley went to the Empty Bottle.

*   *   *

Clava Studios was a conspicuous presence in a very insular Italian/Irish-American neighborhood on the South Side of Chicago.

And so when a troupe of indie-looking folks from god knows where suddenly emerged, moved in, and started making constant construction noise, followed by . . . live music, it was perhaps akin to a suspicious growth emerging on the fabric of the community. Was it a benign cyst or a tumor?

Shit naturally got weird.

Deck describes Bridgeport as a working-class neighborhood—but one with power, as everyone had family members who were police officers, worked for the fire department or sanitation, and all were friends with the mayor, who also lived there.

About a block from Clava sat a (since-evicted) tavern called Jimbo's, which was known as a go-to White Sox bar. After work wrapped up on the album one day, Deck moseyed over for a beer. Deck had personally never met any of the barflies or anyone else there. But as he went up for a shot and a brew, the bartender called him by name and said, "This one's on me," as Sinatra crooned on the jukebox. "You ain't never gonna record anything like this," he recalls the barkeep adding.

Hurley describes the neighborhood as having a perpetually ominous feel. One wonders if the aura at the time, perhaps viewed through an almost David Lynchian kaleidoscope, saturated its way into the music—if it left not a stain, exactly, but a hue. What happened not long after undoubtedly did.

"A bunch of their over-testosteroned mid-teen meathead sons would hang out in the park across the corner from the studio every night in the summertime and burn fires in the garbage cans and hoot and holler and raise hell," Deck recalls.

Objectively, Armour Square Park and the neighborhood at large were no stranger to controversy. As Illinois' *Daily Herald* reported in October 2000, following a White Sox hot streak:

> Jimbo's Lounge at 33rd Street and Princeton Avenue near Comiskey Park embraces White Sox fans and Bridgeport neighborhood locals—such as workers at DiFoggio Plumbing Partners Inc. one block away—who need much willpower to depart without devouring the $3.25 beef sandwich or a daily special.

> Owner Jimbo Levato, 65, has lived in Bridgeport his whole life and doesn't tolerate trouble in his establishment. He also points with pride to all the new homes rising around his place and families returning to the South Side from the suburbs. [. . .]

But despite the friendly appearances, Jimbo's and its neighborhood are fighting an unsavory reputation. [. . .] Jimbo's borders the north side of Armour Square Park, which typically bustles with children playing in the afternoon in Comiskey's shadows. At night, however, the park can be a different story.

Armour Square Park is where black teenager Lenard Clark was severely beaten by three young white men in a racially motivated attack in 1997. The area found itself in an unflattering spotlight again in June, when WMVP 1000-AM sportscaster Bill Simonson and a friend, Ron Bell, said they were beaten by several young thugs near the park following a Cubs-Sox game. Chicago police officer Edward Alonzo said an investigation into the attack on Simonson remains open. He said there are no suspects.

Simonson, 38, and Bell had just left Jimbo's and said they were going to catch a CTA train about five blocks away at the 35th Street stop. Levato said no one at his bar witnessed or participated in the Simonson attack, but its name got dragged through the mud nonetheless. Police have been keeping an eye on Jimbo's on game nights since the Simonson beating. Levato said he's frustrated with the stereotyping of his neighborhood being dangerous, which resurfaced after the Simonson incident. Such talk actually dates as far back as 1969, when the neighborhood was one of the reasons cited for the Sox attracting a paltry season attendance of about 500,000 with a terrible team.

[. . .] Still, a few doors from where powder-blue balloons fluttered heralding the arrival of newborn Rocco Carmen Arcieri, some Jimbo's patrons say there is an element of danger late at night around Armour Square Park. One of them, Bill Clift of Chicago, recalled how some young toughs at the park jumped him when a friend yelled at them after a Sox game in 1993.

"I got whacked in the head with a bottle," said Clift, adding that neither Jimbo's nor the neighborhood had anything to do with his unpleasant experience.

Greg Ratajczack says there was one hard-and-fast rule at Clava: "Don't fuck with the kids in the park. Simple as that, man. Don't do it. They're all locals. They're all connected. Don't fuck with the kids in the park."

You can probably guess what happened next.

*　*　*

Ratajczack remembers coming to work the next day and seeing a look of terror on everyone's faces.

Jesus fuck, Deck recalls thinking.

Brock had fucked with the kids in the park.

Hurley remembers arriving back at Clava the previous night and the van pulling up alongside the park. Brock then headed for the street toughs holding court there.

"When he got out of the van, I was so bummed and so pissed at him immediately, because I was just like, this is the worst fucking idea—but I can't let him go out there by himself," he says.

So Hurley and his dog, Spooky, followed. "I was just so uncomfortable standing there, and just wanted it to be over."

Soon, it was.

"A sucker punch comes, and that happens, and then the next thing you know the bottles are flying, they're trying to hit Spooky with bottles, and we all just kind of scattered in different directions at that point. Luckily, we escaped; obviously Isaac was fucked up badly from that, but he was able to stay on his feet and get back to the apartment."

As for why Brock went over in the first place, there are three basic accounts: Brock's, Deck's, and Ratajczack's. Pick your poison:

In Brock's memory, he didn't smoke cigarettes in the apartment—so that's how he found himself outside that night. And, well, he figured he'd shoot the shit with them.

"My friend [Hurley] was on his way to like, maybe talk me out of talking to them," Brock says. "I think he was more sober and sized it up as, *These people don't want to be your friend, Isaac.*"

Brock asked the group how they were doing—and sans any escalation, got sucker-punched in reply. And it was a hell of a sucker punch.

"I remember it as this: I was walking calmly away. And I hear, 'Fuck you, cowboy.' And they're throwing bottles. My girlfriend remembered it as me *running away*, which is probably true. . . . Honestly, having gotten inside was a pretty big win because the dudes in that park, apparently, I found out later, had a long history of hospitalizing and basically killing people. . . . It wasn't personal. Well, it was personal in so much as there's them, and there's the rest of the fucking world, and the rest of the fucking world can stay out of their park."

For his part, Deck theorizes that Brock might have thought he could deescalate the overall tension between the neighborhood and the studio and fix the issue of the ruffians in the park.

"I think in the back of his mind, he was like, *Given the right opportunity, I can probably smooth some of this over because I'm a nice guy and people like me and I'm unthreatening.* And so they come home after closing the Empty Bottle at like three a.m. And they're looking for a parking place. And the parking place that they find is right next to the park. The goon squad is in the park, having emptied seven cases of beer or something, and they're all gathered around the fire in the fifty-five-gallon oil drum. And Isaac says, 'Look, there's the guys, I'm gonna go talk to them.' And he gets out of his van. And he's talking to them and they're talking to him. And I *think* one of them said, 'You're not from around here, are you?' And he said, 'I've lived here all my life.' And the next thing that happened was the guy threw one punch and broke his jaw in however many places. [Isaac's] intention was, I think, to go over there and just, like, make things cool."[2]

Don't fuck with the kids in the park. I ask Ratajczack if all those warnings might have established a giant red button

---

[2] Worth noting here: all of these interviews took place one-on-one, on different days, in different locations, some completely across the country from one another. I'm not seeking to pit any narrative against another, but rather underscoring the fact that memory is fickle and, again, they all form a mosaic of the truth.

for Brock, who was perhaps uniquely unafraid of a little mayhem.

"You met the guy. He's forty-whatever years old [now]. Imagine every story that you heard—because every story that you heard was *probably* fairly in line. I mean, I'm sure there were some embellishments here and there. But he was a firecracker, we'll say. And he was looking to push buttons, for sure."

Regardless of the cause, there was the effect: in this case, Brock, his girlfriend, and Hurley went to a hospital, which admitted the musician but soon purged him because he didn't have insurance. And so he soon found himself at Cook County Hospital. (As John G. Raffensperger wrote in *The Old Lady on Harrison Street: Cook County Hospital, 1833–1995*, "Cook County Hospital has always been open to all patients, generally poor or destitute, and often alcoholic.") If you've ever been to a hospital in a major city, you know that they offer a rather raucous time. And at the turn of the millennium, the historic Beaux-Arts Cook County—which would close in 2002—was a crumbling, particularly intense place to be.[3]

"Most everyone else was on gurneys, handcuffed to them and suffering from gunshot wounds," Brock says. "And so I was out there quite a while before I got my X-rays since, you know, I wasn't bleeding out."

---

[3] And you can stay the night there on your next trip to Chicago! In 2020, the building reopened, repurposed as two Hyatt hotels, retail shops, medical offices, a food hall, and more. One can't help but feel there's a Modest Mouse song somewhere in there.

A few days after the incident, Ben Massarella recalls getting a phone call from Hurley, who reported that, owing to the marvels of metropolitan triage, no doctor had yet found time to see Brock. So Massarella told Hurley to bring Brock to his home in Valparaiso, Indiana, where there was a hospital four blocks away that was not Cook County. Upon doing so, it was confirmed that, yes, Brock's jaw was indeed broken—and it needed to be wired shut for it to properly heal. So they did, and Brock convalesced at Massarella's house.

At this point in the narrative, I ask Hurley: Throughout that whole period, was Brock terrified that the record was fucked?

Aside from some initial dialogue the night it happened, Hurley says Brock was largely zen about the whole episode.

"During the hospital stay and stuff like that, my recollections are that he was just, you know, the same—which is, he's a person who thrives on the novelty of life. And so all that novelty . . . he was just right there with it."

Back in Seattle, Judy, Green, and Blankenship got word of what had happened, and Judy recalls the latter saying that this was *exactly* what that dark tarot reading had foretold.

Ultimately, the broken jaw is what would go on to make the album—and one wishes they could tell that Armour Square Park hooligan the impact he had on the band's career and music at large with a single, devastatingly executed sneakstrike. Fuck you, cowboy, indeed.

Remember: prior to that night, the music of *The Moon & Antarctica* had been declared finished. But something haunted Brock.

"Honestly, I was a little worried," he says. "When we were done with the basic tracking . . . I remember feeling like, *Shit, this somehow needs a lot. It sounds a little empty*."

As he recuperated, Brock made a request of Deck: Could he get him cassettes of the rough mixes they had recorded? Deck did.

"He listened to it, I guess probably obsessively for a couple of weeks, because he had nothing else to do," Deck says. "And then he got back to me and said, 'Dude, I don't think we're done. I think I have ideas for a lot more.'"

To paraphrase Mike Tyson: everyone has a plan until they get punched in the mouth.

Blending Burgers

After recouping in Indiana, Isaac Brock returned to an eerie post-attack Clava in Chicago. Eric Judy and Jeremiah Green were long gone, and Brock says the kids who attacked him were circling the building and hunting for him.

Moreover, "I overheard old ladies talking about [the attack]—like, 'You know, those fucking guys, Joey and fucking Bob Louie, fucked 'em up! I mean, I don't even think there's a studio in there. I've looked and it's just some drywall.' They were psyched that the boys had fucking got those weird dudes."

So Brock hunkered down and took his (legally prescribed) painkillers. Over the years, Brock has been (perhaps too?) candid about his drug use, casually admitting in interviews to the toll that everything from cocaine to inhalants has taken on him. (As a reminder, right now Brock is wearing a day-glow Modest Mouse–produced shirt covered in mushrooms and just a few years ago released an album that opened with the track "Fuck Your Acid Trip.") So, you might surmise that having a cache of legal drugs would have been an unexpected boon, or at least a silver lining to the debacle. Not so.

"The fog of painkillers . . . it wasn't like there was an addiction or problem. I wasn't taking them to feel fun. As a matter of fact, I actually fucking hate Vicodin and painkillers. That shit makes me edgy and angry. I feel loopy, but kind of easily pissed off, too. So anyways, it definitely doesn't make for the clearest recollection."

(Further on the drug front, Greg Ratajczak—who today works in a dispensary in addition to playing music—remembers the weed during the recordings. Lots of weed. "[Everyone] got so fucking high. And here, I'm in charge of, you know, tens of thousands of dollars worth of gear—you know, ribbon microphones and all sorts of this shit—and I am floating on the ceiling from this Seattle weed that they brought in.")

All the while, Brock's jaw was now wired shut. After one day of vocals. But to define being "wired shut" . . . is that just hyperbole? Modest Mouse mythology that has deepened in the two-and-a-half decades since the album was recorded?

Unfortunately for Brock, it was not. His jaw was wired *shut* shut. He says the process at the time essentially was like getting braces, and the wires were woven throughout all of his teeth and tightened down so he couldn't move his jaw at all, and the only thing he could do was drink fluids. He remembers getting soups from Whole Foods and blending them over and over until he was able to get the macerated mess down, adding, "I put a hamburger at one point in a blender, and I don't remember how that went. I didn't do it again, if that says anything."

As for how well Brock could communicate, Ratajczak finishes the joint he's rolling on a suburban porch and lights it up. He then clamps his jaw tight and mimics Brock's muffled speech, which sounds every bit as bad as it could possibly be. In other words, vocals were off the table until Brock's jaw was healed.

Brian Deck didn't think the record was screwed—he just thought they weren't going to be able to finish it on time. He can't remember if he was the one who had to call Matt Marshall at Epic to break the news, or if it was Sean Hurley. Regardless, Marshall eventually wound up on the line with Brock.

"Our budget wasn't huge," Marshall says. "And I'm just like, *Oh God, now the whole thing's going to be pushed back three months; we just spent X amount of money . . . how am I going to logistically make this work?* And [Brock] was like, 'Don't cancel it. Don't cancel it. Let me just sit in this for a couple days.' I of course was incredibly worried . . . but then the proof's in the pudding. Once I heard it, I was like, *Holy shit. He did it.*"

What everyone seems to unanimously agree on today, explicitly or implicitly, is that the record was better for Brock having been maimed. Because miraculously, it was in this negative space that *The Moon & Antarctica* as we know it took form. It was the point at which, as Brock put it, "You get to fucking really start seasoning the stew."

With largely unrestricted amounts of time on his hands, Brock disappeared into Clava and obsessively layered guitars and sonic terrain of all varieties. Looking back on it, he says with certainty that the record would have been far less dimensional had this not happened—and, well, even if he'd had the time, he would have felt odd spending, say, two entire days making weird sounds on just one track.

THE MOON & ANTARCTICA

Which also has me wondering: Did Brock chip away at the songs like a sculptor working a block of stone, finding their form within as he experimented with backward guitars and assorted audio ephemera? Or did he look at the basic tracks that were completed as a skeleton, and he simply had to graft muscle, veins, and skin onto them to reach the final form he had been envisioning the whole time?

Brock says he knew the vibe he wanted to achieve—and that is what he worked toward, whether he was achieving it through a guitar line or Ben Massarella's subtle percussion, capable of creating an entire soundscape all its own.

Every single sound ultimately seasoned the fucking stew.

As for *how* it all was done, that's where the codeine syrup and that Seattle weed complicate matters.

During our first interview, Brock noted that he and Ratajczak had been the principal players at this stage of the record, and that Deck would only swing by to check on him. About ten minutes later, he added, "It's amazing how differently [Deck] remembers shit than I do. For years, I was under the assumption that just Brian and I worked on the record. That's how I remembered it—and he was like, 'Oh, no, it was just you and Greg the intern. I came back and you guys had basically finished the record.'"

Which, today, is news to Deck.

"Isaac's recollection is that he did it all with Greg?" he asks, seemingly bewildered.

I stammer as I try (and probably fail) to clarify and untangle the threads: well, no, Isaac's recollection is that he did it with *you*, but he says *your* recollection is that he did it all with Ratajczak . . .

"That's funny. No, my recollection is that he and I did it all together, and Greg was around."

In the end, it would seem they both were right: Brock and Deck did it all together, with Ratajczak helping out as needed from his cloud above the room. Memory is a nebulous beast.

One thing that undoubtedly benefited the record: Pro Tools, the multitrack recording software that had come to 24-bit maturation and would soon revolutionize the recording industry in its transition from analog tape to digital. (In 1999, Ricky Martin's "Livin' la Vida Loca" would become the first No. 1 single to be created completely within the software's ecosystem.)

Here, Deck had built the bones of the record on physical tape—but with Pro Tools, the editing process was democratized, and layering was an open door. And Brock walked right through that doorway. By the end of the recording process, Deck says Brock was extremely articulate with what he could accomplish in the program and achieve technically, and how that could aid in the soundscape he had in his mind.

In that lost mass of time, Brock doesn't remember how long he spent at the console with Deck. The producer estimates that, all told, it was about a month's worth of recording ("It wasn't unreasonable; it's not like we were making *Rumours*").

For his part, Ratajczak says the workday started essentially around noon and ran until whenever Brock felt like stopping. He notes that he's a metal guy at heart—and he had never heard of Modest Mouse before they ventured to Clava to record *The Moon & Antarctica*.

"Coming into this, I was like, *OK, this isn't really my thing.* But as it progressed, and as I watched Isaac do what he does, *holy fuck,* man, it's like watching a good chef create a meal. It's just like, *Oh my God*—I tried to remain as present as I possibly could for as much as I possibly could."

Everyone was looking forward to Brock getting his jaw unwired so he could finish the rest of the vocal tracks. But one thing of note was secretly haunting Deck: Brock's signature lisp, a core element of Modest Mouse since day one. When Brock's jaw was wired shut, he didn't have it.

"I was thinking, *Oh, fuck, I'm gonna be the guy who records him for the first time without a lisp. They're gonna unwire his jaw, and he's not going to sound like himself anymore,*" he says with a laugh. "And he thought the same thing; he and I both thought this independently."

Before long, Deck and Brock got their answer.

In October 1999, on the eve of the very first Coachella in Indio, California, Brock got a Leatherman multitool out and began to unwire it himself. In what he dubs a "crazy drunken moment," Judy thinks a member of the band Love as Laughter may have helped out as well.

"I took off shit-tons of tooth enamel doing it, which came back to haunt me later," Brock says. "And then I was in so much pain that I decided, *Oh fuck, I need to take some painkillers for this one.*"

The performance itself consisted of this setlist:

- "3rd Planet"
- "Doin' the Cockroach"

- "Dramamine"
- "Trailer Trash"
- "Paper Thin Walls"
- "Cowboy Dan"
- "Never Ending Math Equation"

It's a safe assumption that the two *Moon & Antarctica* songs probably failed to wow the audience.

"I remember it feeling like just the messiest, most confusing shit show," Brock says.

"They were not invited back for like a decade after that," Hurley tells me later, laughing. "It was a terrible show because he got so drunk to enable that surgery."

The one upside: when Brock opened his newly freed mouth to speak, he still had his lisp. (The downside: his jaw muscles had atrophied.)

Back in the studio, Ratajczak remembers being surprised at how quickly the vocals coalesced and how quickly Brock nailed them. He wonders if Brock having his jaw wired shut added a special element to the performance—an urgency.

"You are here in this town specifically to say something, and document [that] you're saying it. And now you can't. So that's got to be incredibly frustrating as an artist to have to live with that, and to live with your stupid decision on top of that."

His jaw freed, Brock poured vocals atop everything he and Deck had meticulously layered. And then . . . that was essentially a wrap.

Given everything Brock had done to the record while Judy and Green were back home, I wondered: Were they pissed off about the extent of it all?

The opposite: "I was really excited," Judy says.

In a short timeframe, and despite the odds, the band had managed to completely reinvent Modest Mouse.

Aside

Everywhere and His Nasty Parlour Tricks

Isaac Brock, balancing a cigarette in one hand and a recording component of unknown provenance in the other, asks a damn good question: "If you're writing about this record, how do you work in *Everywhere and His Nasty Parlour Tricks*? Because it's basically just the third [part of] the record. Honestly, it kind of largely ties the record together."

A year and a few months after *The Moon & Antarctica* debuted, Epic released this eight-song EP. As the illustrated shaking hands atop its gold cover convey, this is all part of the cosmic bargain first depicted on the cover of the *Night on the Sun* EP.

Everywhere feels as if it pulls some of *The Moon & Antarctica*'s threads to a compelling conclusion. Listened back to back with the manic highs and lows of *The Moon & Antarctica*—especially that damning, thundering finale, "What People Are Made Of"—it serves as a bit of a detox, if not an afterlife. Following a few seconds of a scratchy warm vinyl intro, the beautiful, haunting "Willful Suspension of

Disbelief" eases the record into being. It's Modest Mouse at their most ethereal, perhaps ever.

These songs were recorded essentially at the same time as the rest of *The Moon & Antarctica*—and there is a curious bleedthrough of not just thematic elements but literal audio. Calling to mind Brock's musings on dark matter and parallel universes, the sample that appeared at the end of "A Different City" springs to full life here as the folk-hued, discordant clacking and clanging "3 Inch Horses, Two Faced Monsters," showing the true context of the "I don't know but I been told / you never die and you never grow old" line before it appears on "I Came as a Rat" . . . a song that also features on the EP as the alternately titled "I Came as a Rat (Long Walk Off a Short Dock)" . . . which, to complicate matters further, was the original title of the track when it appeared on the *Night on the Sun* vinyl EP.

For posterity, the track listing is:

1. "Willful Suspension of Disbelief"
2. "Night on the Sun"
3. "3 Inch Horses, Two Faced Monsters"
4. "You're the Good Things"
5. "The Air"
6. "So Much Beauty in Dirt"
7. "Here It Comes"
8. "I Came as a Rat (Long Walk off a Short Dock)"

"Willful Suspension of Disbelief" gives way to the biggest standout on the record, which has gone on to become a

Modest Mouse fan favorite (in my opinion, hands-down one of the band's best songs): "Night on the Sun."

While Brock can't remember where he wrote most of the songs on *The Moon & Antarctica*, he remembers writing "Night on the Sun" at his dad's house in Montana. He estimates it was among the first songs he wrote for the entire *Moon & Antarctica* project, and it was probably created after he got back from his ill-fated Califone practice—"Because I now knew an open tuning." (In this case, that open E that Tim Rutili had shown him. As it happens, Rutili also played guitar on "3 Inch Horses, Two Faced Monsters" here.)

Like the original demos that Modest Mouse presented to Epic, "Night on the Sun" was produced by Phil Ek. Those stark, bone-dry acoustic intro notes, soon joined by Green's delicate cymbal taps, have opened many a Modest Mouse show.

> *So turn off the light 'cause it's night on the sun*
> *You're hopelessly hopeless I hope so for you*
>
> *Freeze your blood and then stab it into in two*
> *Stab your blood into me and blend*
>
> *I eat my own blood and get filled up get filled up*
> *I get filled up on me and end.*

(Housekeeping note: the lyrics above differ from those printed in the liner notes to the *Everywhere and His Nasty Parlour Tricks* EP. These are a version of the lyrics used in the song itself. Perhaps another parallel universe.)

The lyrics take the enigmas of *The Moon & Antarctica* to all-new heights. On the EP, the song plays out over the course of seven-and-a-half minutes, returning to the bounds of Earth in a crescendo where Brock—in shouts— seems to take stock of, and reckon with, our organic mortal position . . . before ultimately accepting (or resigning himself to) it. It's a fitting coda, if not catharsis, to the rage that ends *The Moon & Antarctica*—you know, the whole "water and shit" thing.

Well there's one thing to know about this town
It's five hundred miles underground; that's alright. That's
    alright

Well there's one thing to know about this globe
It's bound and it's willing to explode; that's alright. That's
    alright . . .

Well there's one thing to know about this town
Not a person doesn't want me underground. That's alright.
    That's alright . . .

There's one thing to know about this town
It's five hundred miles underground; and that's OK. That's
    alright. That's alright . . .

There's one thing to know about this earth
We're put here just to make more dirt; and that's OK.
    That's alright. That's alright . . .

The rest of the songs that fill out the EP seem to do a bit of their own time travel[1] to Modest Mouse's past (the flowing acoustic "You're the Good Things," which could have appeared on the band's earlier releases) and even future ("So Much Beauty in Dirt," which wouldn't have felt out of place on *Good News for People Who Love Bad News*). And on the latter point, on "Here It Comes," Judy swaps bass for guitar . . . and Brock picks up the banjo, which he would be doing a lot soon enough for songs like "Bukowski," "This Devil's Workday," "Satin in a Coffin," and the beloved "King Rat."

With "The Air," Brian Deck unites the *Night on the Sun* EP, *The Moon & Antarctica*, and *Everywhere and His Nasty Parlour Tricks* by making trance-inducing abstract poetry of samples from across their collective geography.

One wonders: Why did some of these songs hit the cutting-room floor in the first place?

Brock thinks for a moment.

---

[1] Speaking of time travel, roughly five months before *Everywhere and His Nasty Parlour Tricks* debuted in the wake of *The Moon & Antarctica*, K Records released *Sad Sappy Sucker*, a collection of super early tracks best suited for only the most ardent Modest Mouse fan or the record completionist. At times exuberant, at times nigh unlistenable—especially when it comes to the bevy of "Dial a Song" tracks from Brock's answering machine—the collection's true power is in its archaeological dive into Brock's craft. The songs may not be anywhere in the league of what Brock would showcase a few years later—but they indeed offer a manic preview of it.

"Cowardice or lack of space?" he ventures. "I don't remember why."

He says "3 Inch Horses" should have gone on *The Moon & Antarctica*. Same with "Willful Suspension of Disbelief." The biggest problem: where he would have put them. For the latter song, he says it would have gone where "The Cold Part" appeared, which would have made for "a lighter record" and changed the overall atmosphere significantly.

Regardless: critics were pleased with *Everywhere and His Nasty Parlour Tricks*.

As *The Vancouver Sun* wrote, the EP "is stark, odd, but a sea of gentle calm, filled with winsome space guitar grooves and lyrics."

Per Denver's late *Rocky Mountain News*:

Modest Mouse leader Isaac Brock is nearly untouchable right now, creating songs and sounds that are original and thrilling and yet so familiar that you'd swear you'd heard them before even when you know you haven't. [Neil Young] meets Pink Floyd on the utterly hypnotic interwoven guitars of "Night on the Sun." . . . Brock, bassist Eric Judy and drummer Jeremiah Green aren't afraid to play on and on, yet the result is far from a jam band.

And finally, from Douglas Wolk in *Rolling Stone*:

Everywhere and His Nasty Parlour Tricks is Modest Mouse's sparsest and strangest release, a parched, alien beauty illuminated by a web of little guitar solos that flicker like heat lightning. These one- and two-chord

grooves (plus a blurry instrumental megamix, "The Air")
are blessed with a rhythm section that can tap gently at
a single note until it's driven in far enough. Aside from
a burst of death disco at the end of "You're the Good
Things," the band stays cool and spaced-out, but its dry
throb is the wind beneath Brock's gnarled wings. Songs
drift through the panoramic calm of *Everywhere* until
they run aground, after a minute and a half or five times
that long, while Brock drizzles out vinegary guitar lines
and reels off nightmare images and poker-faced jokes in
his strained lisp.

The EP was dedicated to the memory of Chris Takino, who
cofounded Up Records in 1994. In addition to releasing
Built to Spill's *There's Nothing Wrong with Love* and records
by Caustic Resin, Quasi, and other Pacific Northwest
landmarks, Takino played a big role in launching Modest
Mouse's career. On October 13, 2000, four months to the
day after *The Moon & Antarctica* was released, Takino died
of leukemia at thirty-two. Sean Hurley says Brock was
devastated—and that Takino also had an influence on *The
Moon & Antarctica* in that he was their gateway to bands
like CAN.

One final note on *Everywhere and His Nasty Parlour
Tricks* . . . the perplexing title. It has been debated on Reddit,
bashed in *Pitchfork*'s review of the EP, and on and on. It vexes
the mind: *What does it mean?* There are a medley of guesses
and fan interpretations online. (Just don't ever pull out your
iPhone and fumble your way through a text to a friend
soliciting their opinion on it, lest you may find yourself with

THE MOON & ANTARCTICA

"Everywhere and His Nasty Parkour Tricks.") Ultimately, this brings us to a discussion of lyrical intent and song meanings at large . . . and I apologize to Brock in advance because I know he absolutely does not want to have it.

The Moon & Antarctica

Over the course of two decades of journalism-ing, I've interviewed my fair share of notable people (more writers and artists than anyone would ever care to interact with, equal parts "never meet your heroes," "by all means meet your heroes," and "oh, hey, this purported villain is a pleasant surprise").

I can deal with a cantankerous subject. I can deal with the humble, the timid, or the nonresponsive. I can deal with the self-absorbed, the self-loathing, and the effusively self-promoting. Words are more like objective math than one might think—the right combination and tone can act like numbers, equations that can solve most problems in the course of an interview or everyday life.

My biggest problem when it came to this book and Isaac Brock was I had literally no idea what to expect of him (and thus no idea what to plan for). The band's earliest interviews could be chaotic. In 1996, *Pitchfork*'s first year of existence, Brock informed founder Ryan Schreiber the band had appeared on "Star Search"; at one point Schreiber surmised, "So, everyone's drunk today"; at the conclusion of the interview, Jeremiah Green jokingly (probably?) offered Schreiber some acid.

Elsewhere, Brock simply seemed fatigued by having to talk to the press. As he told *The Reader* in 1998:

> At one point, I decided never to do interviews because I figured I could talk about music or write it. Reporters are always asking me if I care when I get compared to the Pixies or Built to Spill. What am I supposed to say? "That fucking pisses me off, man, I hate that shit"? I don't give a damn. They can compare me to Sade and Prince for all I care.

In 2002, he told *The Seattle Times* that the musical chore he hates doing most is interviews. As he elaborated in 2007 to *Stop Smiling*:

> They read the first article that was ever done on the band, and then ask those questions again and again. It wasn't like the people were even interviewing me because they were at all curious about anything. Some hadn't listened to the records, and I don't think they planned on it. They didn't have any personal interest in what they were asking.

Or, as he told *The AV Club* in 2004:

> I'm not a big fan of the interview. It's a lot of questions I don't have answers for, a lot of questions about the music industry. I make music; I don't give a fuck about all the details of why it's different being on a major label than it is being on an indie label. So go ahead and cross that one off.

Following a last-minute schedule change request from the Modest Mouse camp to punt the interviews for this book a month or so, I found myself boarding a plane to Portland, fearing I could be destined to travel across the country just to hang out in my somewhat seedy Airbnb, located down the hill from Ice Cream Party, with no Brock in sight. But when I walked up said hill to the studio's green and pink facade— topped with no signage but a lone ice cream cone—he pulled up in his SUV at the same time. And he was cordial and polite to not just passersby of all stripes but also the journalist at hand, despite a lifetime of forced interactions with them.

As for Ice Cream Party, Brock acquired the giant 7,755-square-foot property[1] circa 2011/12 as the band worked on *Strangers to Ourselves*: "My whole plot was to make it so that the band could stay here, we could write and record a record and get the fuck out—six-month lease. And I ended up buying it because we didn't finish the record." (The band would famously have an eight-year gap between *We Were Dead Before the Ship Even Sank* and *Strangers to Ourselves*, the longest in Modest Mouse recording history.)

As he occasionally moseys past a handpan drum or xylophone to play a few harmonious notes, he relays personal details and anecdotes, the majority of which can't be printed

---

[1] Fans of Modest Mouse may know of Brock's previously well-publicized taxidermy collection. And there is indeed some here. But Brock says he offloaded a lot of it to spare himself having to explain it to his young kids. Plus, "I don't know how people have fucking taxidermy from like way, way back when. It was probably dunked in poison and shit because moths and stuff find that, and it turns *disgusting*."

here due to sheer tangential invasion of his own privacy. It's refreshing.

He seems to hide little and care little for hiding anything. When he wants something off the record—something he only requests perhaps two times over the course of three days—I honor that, as I do with anyone I'm interviewing. (And to be honest, the things he asked to be off the record were no more slanderous than anything he said on it.)

At one point I bring up those early interviews with *Pitchfork* and others, and Brock smiles and seems a tad loath to admit, "Part of that was just fucking playing it cool, too."

All of this is to say: Brock is (and has long been, sometimes at his own expense) an open book. But still, there are some things that are closed—consciously or not.

* * *

At first listen, the track structure and tone of *The Moon & Antarctica* might seem discordant. To me, it initially nodded at the chaos that governs life and the universe at large. But over the years, I began to see it in a series of four acts:

- In the first, musically—not exactly lyrically— the album begins with an almost sweet, upbeat tone: "3rd Planet," "Gravity Rides Everything," "Dark Center of the Universe."

- Then, it takes a drastically dark turn, first plunging into an abyss with "Perfect Disguise," before embracing said darkness with "Tiny Cities Made of Ashes," the urgent cry of "A Different City," the depths of "The Cold Part" and "Alone Down There," and finally "The Stars Are Projectors," which serves as a bit of a transition from dark to light.

- In its third brief turn, the music feels as if it begins to find redemption with "Wild Packs of Family Dogs" and "Paper Thin Walls," and the somewhat bipolar blend of light and dark on "I Came as a Rat" and "Lives."

- And finally, things backslide into resignation with "Life Like Weeds," culminating in the blazing, rage-filled finale of "What People Are Made Of."

Now, let's acknowledge that all of the above is armchair critical analysis. And that's where books like this can often lose me. Personal interpretation is just that: personal. In other words, it is not universal . . . as books tend to be intended. So I ask for your grace when I dip into (hopefully rare) moments of personal interpretation, and I also ask for your skepticism when it comes to peering beneath the hood of songs, unless the insights come directly from the band.

If you're seeking to unravel the enigma of *The Moon & Antarctica*, the best place to look is not album reviews but the lyrics themselves. I had planned to publish the lyrics to all of the songs from the record in this book, but quickly found myself in the quagmire of music publishing rights at Sony. Despite what you might think, given the amount of (generally awful, often comically incorrect) lyric aggregator/discussion websites out there, song lyrics are notoriously hard (and notoriously expensive) to publish in a formal capacity, despite having the blessing of band management, and so on. So, I opted instead to just get the clearance to reprint the lyrics to a few key songs discussed in this book, exactly as they appear in the liner notes of *The Moon & Antarctica* tenth-anniversary reissue LP, the latest—and perhaps thus currently most "canon"—iteration of the record. (Though, fair warning: in some cases, they differ from what Brocks seems to actually sing.) Divorced from the music, they are a fascinating collection of wordplay and imagery, utterly rich despite often thriving in their simplicity and starkness. Moreover, consciously engaging with them on paper versus regurgitated memory couched in the band's collective soundscape, you might be surprised with what you find, as I was—a new interpretation here, a realization of a twenty-five-year misheard lyric there.

If one needs any convincing of Brock's lyrical prowess, just ask Johnny Marr. Marr cofounded The Smiths with Morrissey, who is often cited as one of the greatest lyricists of his time. Marr temporarily joined Modest Mouse for the 2007 album *We Were Dead Before the Ship Even Sank*, and, as he told *Stereogum* in 2021, "I loved being in the band. There was a brotherhood that is there to this day. Probably the best time of my life. . . . And Isaac Brock is the greatest lyricist I've ever worked with. I've seen him write an amazing song, and then make it better, and then make it better again."[2]

Looking back on *The Moon & Antarctica*, Greg Ratajczak reminds me that he was not an active Modest Mouse fan

---

[2]As for the brilliant interlocking guitar work on that album, "[Marr] plays fluid and I play jaggedy, or like punctuated," Brock told me. "So it worked. I *knew* it would work."

going into the recording—but he was continually blown away by the entire experience. And part of that was because of the lyrics.

"I was wowed by the drum parts, wowed by the bass parts, wowed by the guitar parts, wowed by how the vocals fit in— and wowed by the lyrics," he says. "And I'm not a 'lyrics in music' guy. Hearing these words and hearing these stories told, and how he's painting these pictures where—almost like Tom Waits-style or Bukowski-style—you can smell the room, taste the liquor! You know what I'm saying? I'm a big Tom Waits and Bukowski guy. Here I am, getting to kind of live vicariously through a modern-day Bukowski . . . this out-of-his-mind fucking artist, in the throes of creating his master work."

As for how the lyrics were received when the album was released, one critic from Pennsylvania's *Intelligencer Journal* dubbed them "cryptic, often bewildering." For his part, Brock says he's "pretty tricky" when he's writing lyrics and tends to make sure that he can derive three different things out of them that make sense to him—"because that means people can make nine that make sense to them." (Later, he clarifies that he doesn't sit down and count how many possible interpretations he has in the bag, like a quota—rather, it's all a second-nature process for him.)

I note that the sheer fact that he feels his songs *do* have meaning is a boon to listeners, having once been crestfallen to learn that songwriter Doug Martsch said his Built to Spill lyrics don't really mean anything.

"Music forms lyrics," Brock says, drawing deeply on his American Spirit as the sun catches a column of smoke.

THE MOON & ANTARCTICA

"Which may have been what Doug was trying to say. I've listened to his lyrics. They don't mean nothing. Like, they're fucking downright clever. And sometimes it's hard to piece together an entire story—it's not just like, *Oh, this is because you got in a fucking argument with a mailman. Then at the end of this, you guys resolve your argument.* You know? I think that's a weird thing about fucking lyric writing in general. You don't sit down and try and plan the whole concept. [Well,] some people do—I'm sure Morrissey fucking sat down and did that, but a lot of times, it's a thought that you didn't know belonged to you that's in your head. You're constantly working through 1,000 different things at the same time—it's hard to necessarily pin down how you feel about even this month. You don't just feel one way about it; there's a lot of shit going on. Music is fucking magic. It's goddamn magic, because it can pull shit out of you that actually you didn't know was there. You didn't know you had the answer to your own question. Sometimes I fucking go back and listen to shit, and I'm like, *Oh, that's helpful to me now. I kind of didn't get it when I said it.* You know?"

As for when an artist explicitly spells a song out . . .

"God, when I found out what 'Debaser' by the Pixies was about, when I read that . . . " He trails off, shaking his head. "I'm not doing this to you. I'm just gonna leave it."

When I ask Brock if he sees *The Moon & Antarctica* as a concept album, as some critics have dubbed it, I'm surprised when he readily agrees. Not because I disagree, but rather because of how nebulous the concept of a concept album can be[3] and, well, how precious/pretentious the conversations around concept albums can get in the critical aristocracy.

I don't ask Brock to explain the concept underpinning *The Moon & Antarctica*—but I do inquire if he had a set narrative in his mind for it.

"You know, I'd kind of be bullshitting you if I said I did, because really what I know, specifically, is what I wanted the whole thing to feel like," he says, adding that he's curious about what could come out of the (doomed) session with the recall hypnotist, which hadn't happened yet at this point in our conversations. "I'm hoping that it can get some non-bullshit answers out of me. And I'm afraid that those non-bullshit answers might be shamefully fucking shallow."

In 2000, discussing the album's cover (the original version of which appears on the front of this book), Eric Judy told the website *KindaMuzik*, "It's kind of a riddle, the whole damn thing is a riddle." I later asked him if Brock had ever shared the concept underpinning the record. "I know that Isaac described it to me once, but I can't remember what he said," he said.

As for Brock's lack of memory around the recordings at large, Sean Hurley says he's unique among artists he has met.

---

[3]Consulting *Wikipedia's* entry on the subject—which, yes, I recognize is not the most above-board source of music theory and history—reveals concept albums ranging from Pink Floyd's *The Wall* . . . to Blink-182's *Take Off Your Pants and Jacket* and The Beach Boys' *Surfin' Safari*. (And yeah. I'm aware this is indeed a pretentious footnote, as most footnotes tend to be.)

"He's not your average person," he says. "He's not a person that looks backwards. . . . We don't ever reminisce. We don't ever talk about what happened in the past. He's always about what's happening [right now, in the moment]."

*   *   *

Modest Mouse merchandising manager Rocky Tinder swings by and hands Brock another Chelada, and we agree that it's probably time to break out a copy of the record and go track by track. Brock disappears to go grab an LP . . . but returns empty-handed.

"We don't have one," he says in a mildly hilarious moment. In the temple of Modest Mouse, there isn't a single copy of one of their most iconic albums. Luckily, we both have it on our phones.

He lights a cigarette and cues up the first track.

"3rd Planet"

Everything that keeps me together is falling apart/I've got this thing that I consider my only art of fucking people over.

My boss just quit the job says he goin out to find blind spots and he'll do it.

The 3rd Planet is sure that they're being watched by an eye in the sky that can't be stopped.

When you get to the promise land [you're] gonna shake that eyes hand.

Your heart felt good it was drippin pitch and made of wood.
And your hands and knees felt cold and wet on the grass to me.
Outside naked, shiverin looking blue, from the cold sunlight that's reflected off the moon.
Baby cum [angels] fly around you reminding you we used to be three and not just two.

And that's how the world began.
And that's how the world will end.

A 3rd had just been made and we were swimming in the water, didn't know then was it a son was it a daughter.
When it occurred to me that the animals are swimming around in the water in the oceans in our bodies and another had been found another ocean on the planet given that our blood is just like the Atlantic.
And how.

The universe is shaped exactly like the earth if you go straight long enough you'll end up where you were.

Delicate acoustic notes, followed by doubled guitars, Eric Judy's cerebral bass line, and Jeremiah Green's effortless drums. Everything starts simply enough—a perfectly functional Modest Mouse recording. But then the chorus arrives, and Brian Deck's production begins to make itself clear. Distorted bursts of vocal samples join in. They plunge underwater on the next verse, before Brock's voice poignantly emerges with newfound clarity—"Your heart felt good . . . "

Deck recalls being totally psyched about those different vocal effects, which happened in the mixing. Drawing influence from The Flaming Lips—notably *Transmissions From the Satellite Heart*—he also wanted the rhythm section to have a different presence at various points in the song. "It wasn't so much that I was trying to do what they'd done, just that they'd opened my eyes to being able to approach things in a really different way," he says. "['3rd Planet'] was my chance to really explore that kind of stuff."

The track might seem like one of the more straightforward offerings on *The Moon & Antarctica*, but like "Paper Thin Walls," the production work lurking just beneath the surface brings Modest Mouse to life in all-new ways. In kicking off the album, it provides a bridge between the Modest Mouse that came before and the one that would soon take shape in subsequent songs.

Brock says he always wanted to start the album with "3rd Planet"—though he doesn't remember the recording process behind the track. What he does note is that it introduces an audio throughline: the sustainer guitar that he owned (Ratajczak believes it was a Fernandes rig).

"The sustainer plays an interesting role on this record. It adds a pad to the whole fucking thing throughout it in ways where you might not even notice—it's just ringing and humming through the whole thing," Brock says.

At times, you might mistake those sustained high-pitch drones for Brock's signature move of bending harmonics on his guitar. (Think about all those pinging and ringing accents on "Float On," for example. Today, rather than using a whammy bar or something similar to pull them off, he plays them utilizing the floating bridge on his custom Wicks guitars; for high harmonics, he presses down on the bridge; for low bends, he jams his finger under the bridge to pull it upward.) You might also mistake the sustainer for a device like an Ebow, which creates a similar effect on a single string, or wonder if the sounds were all the work of some guitar pedal wizardry, especially if you've ever happened upon the freight elevator at Ice Cream Party that's loaded with hundreds of stomp boxes. But at this point in time, Brock says he only owned a distortion pedal, a tuner, and a delay. Those haunting hums were all this sustainer guitar—which met an untimely fate.

"I threw it out the window of the Fillmore in San Francisco, slightly drunk. Maybe less than slightly drunk. Maybe more drunk. I threw it out the window of the Fillmore. Exploded it."

Why?

"It disappointed me."

The sustainer wasn't something he initially planned to appear so expansively (and often subtly) on the record—

but when he had all the downtime after getting his jaw broken, he found himself opening up every track and layering it in.

As for the lyrics . . . what's the song ultimately about?

Reading between the lines (or on sites like *songmeanings .com*, where users debate exactly that—and which Brock does not read), there are recurring elements that percolate to the surface: babies.[4] Possibly a miscarriage or related situation. ("Reminding you we used to be three and not just two . . . ")

But the "guilt and love and sex" (per Brock) elements are the interpersonal side of the song. Viewing the track from a macro perspective, it's about "identifying human bodies, or any body, as a self-contained universe or planet," he says.

Conceptually, my favorite part of the song is the end: "The universe is shaped exactly like the Earth, if you go straight long enough you'll end up where you were," followed by a literal return to the beginning of the song, which replays one final time: "Everything that keeps me together is falling apart . . . "

Was that him, Isaac Brock, falling apart?

He says nothing for an extended moment while his cigarette burns.

"No comment."

---

[4]When it comes to the enigmatic "Baby cum angels" line, Brock says that, yes, it is indeed a double entendre—babies-cum-angels, and sperm.

"Gravity Rides Everything"

If "3rd Planet" was a gentle suggestion at where this album was going, "Gravity Rides Everything" dives in headfirst. With those reversed audio bends that introduce the song, alongside staccato skips of unknown origins, it's a veritable planting of a flag that shit is going to get cosmic, and it's going to get weird. It's hard to tell what's backwards and what's forward—and that is perhaps a larger point as it ties back to the notions of time and eternity explored on the record.

Eventually the warm acoustic guitar comes in, and the juxtaposition between the two forms an audio palette all its own, as more guitars later join the mix.

Deck says the song came together a bit like a mosaic.

"'Gravity Rides Everything' was very difficult to play—to perform all the different parts of the song, and to perform them fluidly. So we really constructed that out of bits and pieces, which is part of why it was possible to incorporate so much reverse stuff," Deck says. "I think we got mutually stoked at doing that; all of that character of the song was baked into the construction of it. That wasn't [done] at the mixing phase—it sounded like that the whole time because it was built out of these small loops where we were able to do all these things to them as we went. And we turned a corner there as we put that song together, understanding things that could be done."

He adds that "Gravity Rides Everything" was also probably the point of departure for Ugly Casanova, which was Brock's side project with Tim Rutili, Deck, and others.

The remarkable thing about this song: it's one of the first that Brock wrote—ever. He says it dates back to when he was putting out cassettes in the mid-1990s, and it was originally written on a "horrific" short scale toy guitar that was "barely tuned," and all the coils on the strings had frayed. (For that reason, when the band plays it today, he uses a capo).

He doesn't remember what took him so long to record it—just that he eventually became reaware of it around the time of *The Moon & Antarctica* sessions.

As for the reversed audio elements that appear powerfully here and throughout the album, Brock says that back in the days of recording to tape, he had a tendency to flip reels to reverse them, which was tricky—but in the end, "you have a brand-new song to play to."

And it was all now easier to pull off with the nascent Pro Tools software.

"Isaac in particular really gained a handle on the possibilities," Deck told *Electronic Musician* in 2001, elaborating,

> By the end of making the record, he was able to mastermind some cool maneuvers with plug-ins and Pro Tools. Shifting things back and forth, flipping parts around backwards; he was getting good at knowing what he wanted to hear and knowing how to express it. It wasn't so much that he was mixing, but he could look at a song, understand the musical event that he wanted to make happen, understand the tools at his disposal, relate it in a way that I could understand, and make it happen pretty quickly. That helps you to get a good working rhythm.

Today, Judy looks back fondly on the song—especially the lyrics.

"It has one of my favorite lyrics—and not even just of Isaac's, of anybody's: 'As fruit drops, flesh it sags. Everything will fall . . .' That lyric—it just gives me goosebumps now, even. I've always loved that line for some reason."

The reversed bends in the song occasionally threaten to corrode and fall further out of key—but perhaps that's core to it as well.

"I don't want to fuck this up by saying it wrong," Brock says, "but it's natural to get old, and it's all right. Like, not to say you shouldn't do everything you can to slow that process. But, you know, death and decay are beautiful, too."

Music journalist Jordan Bassett, who dubbed *The Moon & Antarctica*, "hands-down one of the greatest records ever made" in *NME*, would likely agree. "It's so huge in its themes," he says over Zoom from the UK. "And yet it's so concise and so perfectly formed—this kind of huge meditation on life and death. And the idea that everything goes back into the ground—you know, that kind of Buddhist idea almost that nothing is wasted. [All] in a four-minute pop song, which I think is a pretty extraordinary achievement."

Modest Mouse fans who bristled at the band signing to a major label were likely apoplectic when they turned on the TV and saw a Nissan Quest minivan commercial featuring "Gravity Rides Everything," with various women loading surfboards, golf clubs, a horse saddle (?), and more into the vehicle. "Moms have changed," the narrator says as Brock sings and those warped guitars play. "Shouldn't a minivan?"

If people were pissed, they didn't speak a word of it to Brock. He cracks another Chelada.

"I can be a fairly . . . formidable person to come up against, and so when people would try and flip me shit, shit-flipping's my fucking specialty. I mean, if I'm good at one fucking thing, it's that. It didn't really come up much."

"Dark Center of the Universe"

To me, this song is the veritable equivalent of the bone throw from *2001: A Space Odyssey*. From the opening notes and cymbal taps to the reversed guitars, it has always felt like a departure to places beyond.

There is also an interesting dichotomy at play here. The music itself bleeds with cosmic vibes—but the lyrics often remain utterly grounded. ("Well it took a lot of work to be the ass that I am . . . ") That blend of the human and cosmic is perhaps what makes *The Moon & Antarctica* what it is; the daily challenge of being organic matter on Earth (Antarctica) in the midst of the literal chaos of the universe (the Moon).

But shit. I'm interpreting again.

"I have no recollection of writing it," Brock says.

What about recording it?

"No recollection of that."

"Perfect Disguise"

This is one of the darkest Modest Mouse songs ever written, from every angle. Musically, Judy's bass brings an immense weight to the song as it mingles with Brock's guitar and

Ben Blankenship's banjo, before a haunted chorus comes to the fore.

Analyzing Green's drums, the delicate glue that holds everything together, Deck notes that there was no reverb on them—that's exactly how the room sounded. He adds that proportionally, it was built a bit like a double-wide trailer, and it was all hard surfaces—a linoleum floor, drywall everywhere with no wall treatments because there wasn't any time to apply any. By virtue of it being a wide-open room, there was some splash to the sound and a little bit of a reverb trail, and the drums took on their own presence. ("I won't say it was complete happenstance that it sounded that good—I did a lot of studying on how to make a good-sounding room," he adds.)

As for the lyrical content of the song, here Brock is candid. In 1999, Seattle, which had deeply embraced the band early on, would go on to tear itself in half over them. Alt-weekly *The Stranger* released a cover story titled "Immodest Mouse," in which the author described a rape allegation against Brock by a nineteen-year-old woman. Following a night at a bar, the two went back to the apartment Brock shared with Hurley. Brock says the subsequent sexual encounter was consensual. The other party disagreed. The late music journalist Jonathan Valania investigated the allegation in a lengthy *BuzzFeed* article about the band in 2015:

> Hurley remembers hearing Brock in his bedroom next door whispering, "We have to be quiet, or we'll wake up my roommate." Hurley lay awake for a while, and never

heard anything that sounded like someone was in distress. He fell back to sleep. Brock says he and the woman had consensual sex and afterward walked a quarter mile together to the nearby QFC grocery store for some late-night snacks. . . . They then walked the quarter mile back to Brock's house, ate the snacks, and fell asleep. Hurley was up early the next morning working on his computer in the living room. He remembers the woman emerging from Brock's bedroom around 10 a.m. and leaving in a cab without saying anything. "Let me be clear that it is not my point of view to question women who report rapes," says Hurley today. "Sexual violence is rampant, common, and a horrible problem. Having said that, Isaac was shattered. It was a big part of his persona to be someone who stood up for women's rights, and [he] railed against sexual violence."

The woman filed a complaint with the Seattle Police Department, and Brock was interviewed over the phone but was never arrested or charged. Per Valania:

The Seattle Police Department and the King County Prosecuting Attorney's Office expunge files after five years as per the policy for cases where charges were never filed, and therefore a police report no longer exists. "Charges were not filed because there was insufficient evidence of a crime," Dan Donohoe, spokesperson for the prosecuting attorney's office, told me. . . .

"I was really hoping for a trial," says Brock. "Because I was certain the facts would acquit me and this thing would be put behind me. Instead, it's like a dark cloud that follows me wherever I go. I can't outrun it: I doubt I'll outlive it."

To the best of my research, the woman has not publicly spoken about the incident since the original *Stranger* article, and I was unable to track her down.

For his part, during our interviews, Brock did not dance around the subject and brought it up in the first fifteen minutes of the recorder being on. He detailed the background to it and said he had even hired a private investigator at the time. Seattle would come to be momentarily split by those who supported the band and those who supported the person making the allegation, which also played out in the editorial pages of *The Stranger*, with some readers and involved parties accusing the paper of sensationalizing the claim and not doing journalistic due diligence, and others saying it trivialized the subject of rape at large (which can admittedly feel a bit hard to defend with a headline like "Immodest Mouse").

A few people told me that the accuser had recanted the allegation, which some journalists have also reported— though I was also unable to find any official record of that.

Ultimately, no one knows what they experienced in that room except the woman and Brock. But it would create a gap to leave it out of this book because of the impact it had on songs like this one in particular.

Brock says that today, to him, "Perfect Disguise" is no longer about his own experience. Which led me to ask about the influence of the allegation at large. While Brock says it had an impact on the lyrics to this track, had it not happened, the music would still have been the same. "I would have written that same guitar part," he says. "Like I said at one point earlier, the song creates the lyrics. It would have been the same-sounding song, it just wouldn't have had the same words."

"Tiny Cities Made of Ashes"

As "Perfect Disguise" closes, sounds begin to fragment and splinter in reverse, and Judy and Green seamlessly take the wheel. (These subtle transitions remind the listener that this isn't just a strange array of disparate songs but parts of a whole.)

Judy says the driving bass line that defines "Tiny Cities" is the first part of his riff from "Truckers Atlas," which appeared on *The Lonesome Crowded West*. He thinks "Tiny Cities" may have been written in studio as the result of a jam.

"You can obviously tell I'm just playing along," Brock says. "I was along for the ride on that one. Eric and Jeremy together were fucking genius—that rhythm section was fucking incredible. [Though] I hate calling it a 'rhythm section' because it makes it sound like it's separate from the band."

One thing Deck remembers fondly from Green's work on the album—the stick twirling.

"At the time, he could not fucking play drums without twirling his sticks," he says. "It was like a nervous habit between every fucking hit. And it was so funny. I think I considered asking him not to do that—I was like, 'What if the stick goes flying into a microphone or something?' But it was like, no, it sounds great—just do it. I've never recorded anyone else who sounds like that."

He adds that Ben Massarella contributed a significant amount of percussion to the track. Notably, Deck remembers a big plastic ball that seemed to have once been part of a commercial light fixture (he's not entirely sure where it came from—perhaps the truck wash). There was a hole at the top, and they would hang a microphone inside it and then whack the ball, which would generate a sound like a basketball on a gym floor, featuring prominently in the song.

"He did a lot of things that are small, but they create this dimension, this depth to it," Deck notes.

Massarella says Deck developed a knack for editing out the attack of different sounds—meaning, in this case, the moment when that ball was struck—which further detached the remaining audio from reality, leaving listeners unsure where a sound truly originated. When it came to his contributions on the record at large, Massarella adds, there was no real structure to them, and the process was loose—given that the Perishable label was right next door, Brock would occasionally ask Massarella to try something on a given track, or Deck would invite him to tinker around on some ideas.

As for the violins here, Deck remembers going upstairs to the apartment and listening to a bunch of Marvin Gaye, realizing "*That's* what we're trying to do," and heading back to the studio to lay down a bunch of octave violins. As they swell up and down, Brock—his voice doubled here—aligns his signature harmonic bends with reversed guitar, everything going forward and backward. To Green's pulsing beat, the bass line is relentless and unceasing, a facsimile of time itself.

When it comes to the title, Brock says "Tiny Cities Made of Ashes" is a line that his friend Sean Hurley had written down on a piece of paper—but he has no recollection of why (it might have been referring to ashtrays). Either way, he co-opted it, and it has since become one of his favorite Modest Mouse songs.

Lyrically, he says it's not so much a story as it is a vibe.

But, "I'm gonna leave you hanging on this one, man. Because on some level, songwriting doesn't work as linear as storytelling. . . . When you buy a book, it doesn't have a soundtrack. Because the book itself can stand on its own, or should be able to. [With music,] you're allowed to paint a fucking pretty vague picture lyrically, and therefore allow it to be a lot more things—even to yourself. With a book, I bet 90 percent of [people] never fucking reread it. They know it—they know the story that was told. As though I'm not in the band, I can listen to a song like 'Tiny Cities' and get a fucking different thing depending on where I'm at in my life, what's going on that fucking day, and make it make sense to me in a new way every time. And that's the goddamn beauty of music."

One tangential coda regarding the little collage of double acoustic guitars and reversed audio that closes the track and provides a transition to "A Different City"—for some reason, it's not accounted for in the song times that are printed on the disc and CD. Nor is the transition at the end of "Perfect

THE MOON & ANTARCTICA

Disguise" or the outro to "A Different City." The actual length of the songs has always been printed without them, from the original 2000 release to the 2004 reissue and the tenth-anniversary edition in 2010.

"A Different City"

While *NPR* would dub "Tiny Cities" "like a lost Talking Heads classic reworked by a thrash metal band," they summed "A Different City" up as evoking "New Wave darlings such as Devo and the B-52's."

Something that may surprise you: no one associated with this recording seems to actually like it.

"'A Different City' was slightly more metal than I ever expected it to be," Brock says. "As a matter of fact, that's kind of driven me crazy ever since I put it out—*is this too metal?*"

The song launches into form with Brock's searing guitar line, heavily doused in a spacey metallic effect, perhaps a flanger or phaser, perhaps with some chorus added. Brock says he didn't own any such pedals at the time, and it might have been an effect Deck added. He vaguely remembers feeling unsure about it. ("I had a real hard-on for hating the way that chorus and flange and shit sounded because of what happened to grunge. I'm a grunge purist—like, I like Mudhoney and Tad and things. When it's Nirvana and it sounds like they're underwater . . . it just sounds so cheesy to me.")

If you've ever thought the recording feels slightly different than the rest of the album, you'd be spot on. Deck recorded an original version with the rest of the songs and says he mixed it, and everyone called it done. But a couple of months later, he says, Brock called and asked him not to take offense, but he just wasn't into the version they had captured—it lacked the presence or power he had intended for it to have, and he didn't think Clava was capable of making the song sound the way it ought to.

So the band came back to Chicago and spent two days recording a new version in a studio across the hall from what would eventually become Deck's Narwhal Studios in Wicker Park. Deck had never worked there and didn't know the rooms—"and frankly, the live room in that studio sounded like ass. It sounded dead as shit. And we couldn't get a drum sound, I couldn't get good guitar sounds—it didn't come out well. And it is the version on the record." Judy says he also prefers the original version (if you're curious, look up "Moon & Antarctica demos" on YouTube, and you can hear something more akin to how the track originally sounded).

As for that aforementioned outro, the folksy snippet from "3 Inch Horses, Two Faced Monsters" that comes back on "I Came as a Rat"—"I don't know, but I been told, you never die and you never grow old"—Brock says he feels like it's an old blues line. Moreover: "It's creepy as fuck." Which is perhaps a good transition here.

"The Cold Part"

When Modest Mouse arrived in Chicago to record *The Moon & Antarctica*, "The Cold Part" didn't exist.

Rather, one of the album's most desolate tracks—which today feels wholly critical to the record—was invented whole cloth by Brock and Co. in the lost miasma of time after he got his jaw broken. Though it's an abyss of a song, it also underscores the beautiful violin work of Tyler Reilly, who appears on "Dark Center of the Universe," "Tiny Cities Made of Ashes," "The Stars Are Projectors," "Lives," and "Life Like Weeds."

And it further showcases the textured landscapes of Massarella's percussion. Brock says his only memory of recording the song is Massarella having bundles of drumsticks rubber-banded together; when you listen closely, you can hear them clacking and mistake it for delay.

As for all those little squeaks and squawks, Ratajczak says they're the result of Massarella holding a vibrating dildo being played into a contact microphone through a Space Echo tape delay unit. Ratajczak also received a performance credit for the swell of dissonant guitar toward the end of the song.

I might venture that this is the spookiest song on the album—were it not for the next one.

"Alone Down There"

How do How do you do.

My name is you. Flies they all gather round me and you too.

You can't see anything well. You ask me what size it is not what I sell.

The flies they all gather round me and you too.

I don't want you to be alone down there. To be alone down there. To be alone.

The Devils apprentice he gave me some credit he fed me a line and I'll probably regret it.

I don't want you to be alone down there. To be alone down there. To be alone.
Ah
I don't want you to be alone down there. To be alone down there. To be alone.

We're halfway through the tracklist, and Brock has switched from the Cheladas to a liquid of unknown origin in a metal cup.

He cues up the song, and the sinister-sounding interlocking guitar and bass begin, almost like the metronomical passing of a clock's hands. A chorus of giggling Brocks joins in before the song erupts into an almost desperate cry: *I don't want you to be alone down there.*

One thing you've probably guessed from the lyrics: Brock says this song is perhaps the most direct link to the entity he felt pass through him.

He draws on his cigarette and listens to the song for an extended moment, then exhales. It's about "not wanting someone to be alone in hell," he says. "Or alone in the worst place on Earth. Also, I went back and forth about not wanting the devil to be lonely."

We talk about the difficulty of recording claps for a moment (given the signature burst of them that appears at 1:37 in). But then he pauses again.

"Sometimes I'm just answering questions with an answer that might work," he says. "My whole 'alone down there in hell' thing . . . it's off the cuff . . . I'm sorry. I've made my entire career pretty much about not explaining these songs, and now I'm trying to do it. And maybe that's why I don't remember. But it was important to me to not explain these songs."

The reason why is simple.

"Ruins songs," he says, shaking his head slowly. "There's so much more you can take away from a song if someone doesn't tell you what you're supposed to take away."

He hits "play" on the song again and seems to listen intently.

"It's a little easier to explain this way: It's about evil. True evil lives within and . . . what parts of you are evil? And can you tell the difference? . . . It's just about pure evil. And yourself."

This makes me ponder duality and the different layered vocal tracks—the vulnerable-sounding main vocal and the whispered lyrics atop it, rotating in and out on stereo during the first verse before coalescing into a unified screaming chorus.

Deck says he believes it was his idea to have Brock double them. "When I thought that a song needed to feel creepy, I would ask the singer to exhale completely before they began singing so they would have no breath left to support what they were doing. And it would sound like they were whispering in your ear."

Deck had spent time in Seattle doing preproduction with the band before the main sessions, and while there, he heard "Alone Down There" and thought it might have commercial legs—but he felt it was missing a part. So he says he wrote an outro for the song, and the band played it—and used it on the record. ("I couldn't believe it," he says.) With its shift in tone and overall vibe, it feels a bit bipolar . . . but in the best of ways. And it feels utterly at home on *The Moon & Antarctica*.

"The Stars Are Projectors"

In the last second of life they're gonna show you how.
How they run this show. Sure. Run it into the ground.

The stars are projectors, yeah.
Projectin our lives down to this planet earth.
The stars are projectors, yeah.
Projectin our minds down to this planet earth.

Everyone wants a double feature they wanna be their own damn teacher, and how, all the stars are projectors, yeah.
Projectin our lives down to this planet earth.

It's all about moderate climates you gotta be cold and be hot for sure.
It's all about the moderate climates you wanna be blessed and be cursed for sure.

All the stars are projectors yeah. Projectin our lives down to this planet earth.

All the stars are projectors yeah. Projectin our lives down to this planet earth.

Everyone wants a double feature they wanna be their own damn teacher, and how, all the stars are projectors, yeah.

Projectin our lives down to this planet earth.

You've got the harder part you've got the kinder heart and [it's] true.

I've got the easy part I've got the harder heart ain't this true.

Right wing, left wing, chicken wing.

It's built on findin the easier ways through.

God is a woman and the woman is, an animal that animals man and that's you.

Was [there] a need for creation? that was hidin in a math equation and that's this.

WHERE DO CIRCLES BEGIN?

Having snaked in and out of the record, all roads from Brock's sustainer guitar lead here. And when it leaves the background and announces its presence at the start of the track, it's almost frightening—a high-pitch bending resonation that could cut glass. Green's thunderous drums come pounding in, and all the raging Brocks are back, a contained cacophony of undulating voices and sounds that eventually give way to multiple evolutions in tone and tempo.

How does a nearly nine-minute song like this even get written in the first place?

It's Brock's favorite track on the record, and he says it all spawned from the core riff of the first verse ("In the last second . . . "). Then, it's a bit akin to a family tree from there. "That gives birth just by its being there with your brain—they make sweet, sweet fucking love and make a baby of the next part. And that's kind of how this one happened."

You might think the recording of "The Stars Are Projectors" involved capturing the many parts individually and then stitching them together in Pro Tools. Not so. Deck recalls that the band was having a difficult time playing through the song, and they were getting frustrated. Moreover, to circle back to the setting of all this, their neighbors in residential Bridgeport were not exactly fans of the studio. It was around 8:00 p.m., and Deck was nervous about tracking things too late, having just come off making construction noise well past midnight for weeks.

"So I said, 'Well, let's dim all the lights, smoke a bunch of dope, and take one more run at this thing. And if we don't get it, then we'll just come back tomorrow.' So we did that. And they went out there and played the version that's on the record. And I remember just being *floored*. The flow of it, and the perfection of the dynamic and the way that everybody pulled it off—it was *all there*. The layers weren't there. But the guitar melody was. It was joyful. It was so fucking cool. To this day, one of the coolest things I've ever seen in a studio. They completely encapsulated the expression of what that song was at its essence. And the layers just added to that, texturally."

Ratajczak was also in the room.

"It was one take," he marvels. "Sitting there and watching these songs be performed, [I was just] kind of mesmerized at how good they were as a band. Truly a band that worked really hard, toured a lot, knew one another really well, and had a great understanding of one another's place in the music sonically."

As the delayed guitars dance around at the song's crescendo, Brock asks one final lyrical question that feels crucial to the song and the album at large: *Where do circles begin?* The notion of infinity and the paradoxes therein, when applied to endless subjects (perhaps matched in audio with those reversed guitars that toy with time), coupled with human polarity (perhaps matched by the myriad vocal overdubs), make "The Stars Are Projectors" not just the best track of the whole record, in my opinion, but perhaps the key to it all.

And from a craft standpoint, it appears exactly where it should for maximum effect, says Bassett.

"The great masterstroke in terms of this record is having 'The Stars Are Projectors' pretty much bang in the middle of it. It's this incredibly expansive track which gives the album so much room to breathe, and it makes the album feel so spacious and meditative." Moreover, viewing this record side by side with the already thematically rich *Lonesome Crowded West*, "the themes on *The Moon & Antarctica* are just so much *bigger*, aren't they? The universe and life and death—it's just a much, much bigger, more expansive record in every way."

. . . *Where do circles begin?* By the time the final twinkling bars play, it's something you've actually had the space to ponder.

"Wild Packs of Family Dogs"

After the cerebral heights of "The Stars Are Projectors," the humble acoustic "Wild Packs of Family Dogs" (which Phil Ek recorded at Jupiter Studio in Seattle) serves not exactly as a palette cleanser but a return to Earth.

"You [can't] write a grand fucking record about the universe without talking about the tiny neighborhood," Brock says.

After Modest Mouse played "Wild Packs of Family Dogs" during a 2004 *Austin City Limits* taping, Brock concluded, "And that's the end of that true story told by a liar."

And, well, he wasn't lying: "That basically really happened," he says of the song.

Sure, his sister wasn't eaten by dogs. But Brock says that when he was growing up, people who didn't want their dogs anymore would just release them, and they eventually formed packs—and a pack once dragged off one of his friends. (They got him back.)

"They would try to grab kids off porches and shit," he says. "Probably a lot of fun for them. I definitely didn't want to follow 'Stars Are Projectors' with something dense. So, an acoustic guitar and a weird-ass kinda semi-true story."

Objectively, one wouldn't think a song about wild dogs dragging children off and then being rewarded as good boys in heaven would be a moment of grounding . . . but again, that's *The Moon & Antarctica*.

"Paper Thin Walls"

With the album momentarily back on terrestrial ground, Brock says "Paper Thin Walls" derives from the existence of living in a studio apartment with strangers separated by nothing more than half-inch-thick drywall.

On face value, "Paper Thin Walls" sounds like a straightforward pop song, if not a hint at what was to follow on *Good News for People Who Love Bad News*. But under the hood, there's a lot going on.

Some of the more interesting elements: the African agogo bells that Deck bought at a percussion shop in Chicago, which can be heard throughout the song; Tim Rutili's backing vocals; and the chimey guitars that accentuate the two parts of the song where Brock sings "Tow the line to tax the time," which was all Blankenship. Brock says Blankenship set up a bunch of guitars in open tunings, and then he would walk by them during the chorus and strum each one.

"That was pretty clever. It could have been done with one guitar multiple times, but he kept the craft. He was a nice dude. We were young and I think he got on my nerves at some point, and I think he knows it; I remember at one point getting an apology letter from him just kind of explaining, 'I was kind of being a kook.' I never responded or said, 'but you were cool.' But he was cool."

Deck thought the song should be a dominant radio single, but he was flummoxed by its structure because the verse starts wildly catchy . . . and then the song gets less so as it continues.

"It had this structure that was at odds with the commercial viability and the good feeling of the verse," he says. "And I didn't know how to fight that. . . . I don't know if I could have cracked the code any better, if it could have been more of a 'focus track,' as they say. But you get celebrated for having made a song like that nowadays. Back then it was just a frustration for the record company."

Which makes me wonder: Did he have any fears about turning in the record at large to Epic?

"Well, I had nothing but fear. Matt [Marshall] helped me feel OK about it simply by being around and having enthusiasm for it. I don't remember him saying anything like, 'I don't hear a single . . .'"

Instead, Deck says he remembers positive feedback and enthusiasm—and a general feeling from Brock that he had made something he could be proud of.

Still, "It would have been nice to achieve basically what 'Float On' achieved for them one record later," Deck says. "To have been a part of achieving that on this record would have been like if the Oakland A's had beat Boston."

"I Came as a Rat"

Well I ain't sure but I been told
He's baking cakes inside our souls
Stayed awake took a nap
Got myself my bottles back
I'm breakin them out on the street
Walkin round in my bare feet
I do not need you to tell me that I am not a cat
I caught a ride we caught some air
He's never gonna cut his hair
It takes more time to make a fake
We night swam down in the lake
Washed the dirt off our intentions
Prattle on 'bout bad inventions

I came as Ice
I came as a whore
I came as advice that came too short
I came as gold
I came as crap
I came clean and I came as a Rat
It takes a long time but god dies too
But not before he'll stick it to you
Well I don't know but I been told
You never die and you never grow old
Uh oh!

I came as a call
I came as flat
I came too soon so I came back
I came as flowers

I came as nice
I came as dirt and I came as its price
It takes a long time but god dies too
But not before he'll stick it to you
I don't but I been told you never die and
you never grow old
Uh Oh!

As far as dualities go, "I Came as a Rat" begins with a brilliant set of them—the tinny, scratchy octaves ringing out from a tiny amplifier built into a cigarette pack that Brock had, and his fuller, almost metronomic notes playing over it. Simultaneously, double vocal tracks give way to an almost Western film–sounding chord progression. After a mere two minutes, everything crescendos to a beautiful jam featuring the return of Brock's cigarette pack amp, which sounds at times like a pissed-off coven of bees, as Green's drums frolic about in inventive ways, and the reversed audio returns as well.

"I Came as a Rat" has always felt like one of the most enigmatic tracks on the album, in both structure and lyrical content. And I'll spare you my interpretation of it and encourage you to find your own.

"Lives"

*Everyone's afraid of their own life if you could be anything
you want I bet you'd be disappointed, am I right.*
*No one really knows the ones they love. If you knew
everything they thought I bet that you'd wish that they'd just
shut up.*

*Well you were the dull sound of sharp math when you
were alive. No ones gonna play the harp when you die,
and if I had a nickel for every damn dime I'd have half
the time.*
Do you mind.

Everyone's afraid of their own lives.
*If you could be anything you want I bet you'd be disappointed
am I right? Am I right.*

And it's our Lives.

*It's hard to remember it's hard to remember We're alive for
the first time*
It's hard to remember were alive for the last time
*It's hard to remember its hard to remember to live before
you die.*
*It's hard to remember its hard to remember that our lives
are such a short time*
*It's hard to remember its hard to remember when it takes
such a long time*
It's hard to remember its hard to remember

My moms god is a woman and my mom she is a witch
I like this

My hell comes from inside comes from inside myself
Why fight this.

Everyone's afraid of their own lives if you could be anything
you want I bet you'd be disappointed am I right.

To me, "Lives" has always mirrored the often simultaneously soaring and plummeting emotions of life. It begins with a cold, dark acoustic intro[5]—and then drastically evolves into a gentle, delicate composition perfectly accented by Tyler Riley's violin.

At Ice Cream Party, Brock listens and drinks. He contemplates. And he seems to really listen and perhaps hear it anew.

"I think this is one of the most beautiful fucking things I've ever heard," he says, shaking his head, seemingly disarmed and devoid of sarcasm. "It made me want to tear up. . . . Beautiful. Sorry. . . . That does not for a book make."

And then, in the song, there's a realization, a regression—the music returns to its dark intro. The guitars reverse.

Where do circles begin?

---

[5]You should also listen to the version that appears on the *Night on the Sun* EP, which is even more stark.

"Life Like Weeds"

And in this life like weeds
You're just a rock to me

I could have told you all that I love you
And in the places you go you'll see the place where you're
from
I could have told you all that I love you
And in the faces you meet
You'll see the place where you die
I could have told you all that I love You
And on the day that you die you'll see the people you'd met.
I could have told you all that I love You
And in the faces you see you'll see just who you've been
I wish I could have told you all

In this life like weeds
Eyes need us to see
Hearts need us to bleed
In this life like weeds
You're a rock to me
I know where you're from but where do you belong
In this life like weeds
You're the dirt I'll breath
In this life like weeds you're a rock to me

All this talkin all the time and the air fills up up up
Until there's nothin left to breath
And you think you feel most everything
And we know that our hearts are just made out of strings
to be pulled,

strings to be pulled
So you think you've figured out everything
But we know that our minds are just made out of strings to
be pulled,
strings to be pulled
All this talkin all the time and the air fills up up up
Until there's nothin left to breath
Up until there's nothin left [to] speak
Up until the better parts of space.

Speaking of haunting—that's how Judy describes "Life Like Weeds."

And it indeed gets there. But first, it's like a splash of ice-cold water to the face after "Lives." It nearly makes me jump every time I listen to the record, even though I know it's coming—that clacky guitar is like an attack, perfectly balanced with the spacey second guitar interweaving with Judy's bass.

Then the band plays with time, and things turn downright orchestral. (As for all the talk of deities, the devil, and the universe . . . what is music but playing with time, especially in the absence of that same control in the bedlam of life?) It's a song that takes its time, but somehow wastes no time.

If "The Stars Are Projectors" is the biggest moment on the record, "Life Like Weeds" is perhaps the second. Like

"Stars Are Projectors," it defies the verse/chorus/verse/chorus/bridge/etc. traditional song structure and, well, song structures period. At the same time, thanks again to the glue of Green's drumming, it feels utterly organic.

Here, the chorus of sustainers is also back. At least I think it's the sustainer. It could be an Ebow. A harmonic. Something else. Everyone, like me, probably feels they have the record figured out—but it's an album that generally continues to prove you wrong, in the best of ways.

For instance, I always assumed the whole "rock" thing was a positive—as in a constant, a fixed anchor.

"'In this life like weeds, you're just a rock to me' . . . which is to say, I'm worthless and you're nothing but in my way," Brock says. Then he flashes a devilish smile. "I just made that up by the way. No idea what I meant when I wrote it. But that's the fun of fucking music, is *I* get to decide what it is every time I listen to it. Every single fucking time I listen to any of this stuff or anyone's music, I'm like, *Oh, now I get it! Oh my, I never got it before—I thought I'd gotten it the last 100 times perfectly, but this time I get it*. And I didn't, because the next time I get it again."

To that end, music critic Jordan Bassett says part of why the album is so brilliant is because the lyrics are so porous.

Ultimately, for Deck, "I think the record is a really great snapshot of a guy with a very unique worldview," he says. "Definitely unique in terms of songwriters operating in indie rock at the time. And more than any [song] being specifically about anything, I think it's a point of view—it's a Brockian point of view that is discernible."

"What People Are Made Of"

Rag weed tall better hope that his ladder don't crack
Or he'll hit the ground low, hard and out of his back
At the Battle at the bottom of the ocean, well the dead do
rise
You need proof I got proof at the surface you can watch em
float by
Way in back of the room, there sits a cage
Inside it's a clock that you can win if you can guess its age
Which you never can do cuz the time it constantly changes
For luck or lack
I guess that is the saying
On the first page of the book of blue it read
"If you read this page [then] that'll be your death"
By then it was too late
And you wound up on an island of shells and bones that
bodies had left
And the one thing you taught me
'bout human beings was this
They ain't made of nothin but water and shit.

All roads on *The Moon & Antarctica* lead here—and if it takes you by surprise, that's OK, because it's a bit of a twist ending.

It begins with Brock, off mic, seemingly saying, "What's up? Make love?" . . . which, after a pause, he somewhat sheepishly admits to me was intentional and not an accidental capture.

"It was very intentional because shit was about to get dark," he says.

And it does.

Green's intro follows, punctuated immediately after by guitars whose strings sound not exactly like they're being played but mangled. You can tell how hard Brock is hitting them as they scream and struggle toward higher frets. They're distorted, but not drowned in distortion; rather, they're being ground to an extreme.

When Brock starts singing, his voice is distorted too. After a minute and twenty-five seconds of intensity, the guitars drop out, and it's just Green and Judy—whose bass has now become distorted. An acoustic guitar eventually frolics into the mix, and you can tell it's all collectively building to something massive.

And it does.

And the one thing you taught me 'bout human beings was this

Brock then roars.

They ain't made of nothin but water and shit. All right.

And then it ends. It's an explosive, terrifying finish that completely captures a vibe. (Whether the "all right" is a note of finality or a question, I'm not sure. Though if it is the latter, it's perhaps one answered on *Everywhere and His Nasty Parlour Tricks*.)

It's unexpected. Unconventional, given the sonic ground laid before it on the record. But Deck loves it.

"It sounds really raw. It just sounds like the trio playing a live show with maybe a couple of guitar overdubs," he says. "I feel like I'd rather end a record with an exclamation point than an ellipsis."

It has always felt to me like kindred spirits with the enigmatic, shocking ending of the aforementioned *Blood Meridian*, which is perhaps fitting, given that Brock said he finished rereading it around the time Modest Mouse recorded *The Moon & Antarctica*.

In the book, after a time jump from its narrative, the nameless protagonist finds himself in a saloon with a bear trained to dance to an organ. A patron shoots the bear dead—then, a force of utter chaos in the book, Judge Holden, emerges and launches into an unsettling soliloquy that underscores his general worldview:

A man seeks his own destiny and no other, said the judge. Will or nill. Any man who could discover his own fate and elect therefore some opposite course could only come at last to that selfsame reckoning at the same appointed time, for each man's destiny is as large as the world he inhabits and contains within it all opposites as well. The desert upon which so many have been broken is vast and calls for largeness of heart but it is also ultimately empty. It is hard, it is barren. Its very nature is stone . . .

I tell you this. As war becomes dishonored and its nobility called into question those honorable men who recognize the sanctity of blood will become excluded from the dance, which is the warrior's right, and thereby will the dance become a false dance and the dancers false dancers. And yet there will be one there always who is a true dancer, and can you guess who that might be?

Not long after, he murders or otherwise does something horrible to the protagonist in an outhouse (it's not specified, which is ominous for a book that vividly describes babies hanging from trees). He then returns inside—and in a thunderous, unexpected conclusion, he dances:

He never sleeps, he says. He says he'll never die. He bows to the fiddlers and sashays backwards and throws back his head and laughs deep in his throat and he is a great favorite, the judge. He wafts his hat and the lunar dome of his skull passes palely under the lamps and he swings about and takes possession of one of the fiddles and he pirouettes and makes a pass, two passes, dancing and fiddling at once. His feet are light and nimble. He never sleeps. He says that he will never die. He dances in light and in shadow and he is a great favorite. He never sleeps, the judge. He is dancing, dancing. He says that he will never die.

Ultimately, Brock says "What People Are Made Of" is the most definitive statement of the entire record.

Aside
Jeremiah Green

Founding Modest Mouse drummer Jeremiah Green died unexpectedly from cancer on December 31, 2022, just a couple weeks before Bloomsbury green-lit this 33 1/3. His loss reverberated through almost every interview conducted for this book—and his voice is the one true missing piece of it.

Isaac Brock described his musical sync with Green as "otherworldly" and said that after his memorial, the only thing he wanted to do was pick up the phone to chat about how strange it had been to run into everyone there—but the person he'd wanted to call was Green.

In the void of Green's presence here, I'm reprinting writer Michael Rietmulder's look back on his life (with minor edits, only for space). It underscores a point Brock made early on in this book about the sudden displacement of memory, and out of all the outlets that covered Green's passing—from *The New York Times* to *Vanity Fair*, *Billboard*, *CNN*, *USA Today*, and even the likes of *TMZ*—it uniquely offers a keyhole glimpse into the person Green was, as told by some of those who knew him best.

"Remembering Jeremiah Green, Modest Mouse's Soft-Spoken 'Rudder'"

by Michael Rietmulder
The Seattle Times, March 1, 2023

It was one of those Showbox nights when the excitement spills out onto the streets, practically radiating from the marquee's glow. Hometown fans wrapped around the block across from Pike Place Market as Modest Mouse was set to begin a three-night stand performing their seminal album *The Lonesome Crowded West* days before Thanksgiving.

The Issaquah-formed indie rock giants had burned through the same beloved songs in the same beloved room roughly a year earlier for a one-off charity event. But last fall was different. The band sounded fiercer and tour-mode tightened in front of a more dedicated crowd that included plenty of friends and family, including Phil Ek, who helped produce the Seattle classic twenty-five years ago.

"Teeth Like God's Shoeshine" and "Doin' the Cockroach" cut like a knife fight while frontman Isaac Brock barked and spat his narrative bus bench poetry through splintering guitars. Jeremiah Green's buoyant percussions—that frequently lift and propel Modest Mouse songs in unorthodox ways—bounced the sold-out crowd like a tattered basketball on the Showbox's famously springy floor.

It wasn't so much a nostalgia fest as a white-knuckle service to one of the Pacific Northwest's most treasured indie rock documents.

What no one knew at the time was that that Showbox run would be Green's last local performances. The band's idiosyncratic drummer and founding member died less than six weeks later. Green, who would have turned forty-six on Saturday, was diagnosed with cancer in his throat in September. While rehearsing in Missoula, Brock nearly canceled the tour entirely, but according to Green's family, the drummer was determined to play some of the dates before starting chemotherapy in December. Green lost so much weight during the treatment that eventually his body was no longer able to fight and he died Dec. 31.

"We had no idea that he was going to pass away," says Adam Green, Jeremiah's brother, who was at the show.

"Cancer's always finicky so there's nothing 100% guaranteed. But I made sure to pay extra special attention to him [that night]. I remember the band just played their encore and they were gonna walk offstage and somebody tried to talk to me and I waved 'em off because I wanted to make sure that I watched him walk off the stage, because it could have been the last time. And I was right."

Green—whom Brock describes as "essentially my brother" and "probably the greatest natural artist I've ever [expletive] met"—was a soft-spoken, kindhearted father and husband; an inquisitive and wildly creative artist and self-taught drummer who played by his own rules, transcending styles and mediums. Two weeks ago, friends and family gathered in Port Townsend, where he'd long made his home, for a private memorial celebrating the life and legacy of the drum-lesson dropout who became one of the most impactful figures in Northwest indie rock. A quiet giant of Seattle's post-grunge indie rock boom, Green's outlived by the mark he left on the community and the many people he touched.

"Play Like You Wanna Play"
The Green brothers spent part of their childhood as skateboarding misfits in Moxee, a small town outside of Yakima, where they were "the only ones listening to The Smiths and The Cure, Sex Pistols, things like that," says Adam, a former DJ at 107.7 The End. After moving to Kirkland, within striking distance of Tower Records, it got easier for their mother, Carol Namatame, to track down albums by the "obscure bands from England" the younger Green, who went by Jeremy then, wanted for his birthday.

Music—specifically *loud* music—was a constant in their home and something the family connected over. Primarily a single mother working multiple jobs, Namatame says she didn't have time to get the boys involved in sports. But on the weekends, she'd load her pickup with kids and drive them to all-ages shows at venues like the Velvet Elvis, OK Hotel or the Old Fire House in Redmond—many of them stages Green would eventually play.

At twelve years old, the left-handed Green, who supposedly wouldn't hold his sticks correctly, briefly took drum lessons until the teacher insisted he had no future with the instrument.

"The drum teacher took me aside and told me that he was just never going to be able to play drums, so I was basically wasting my money and maybe he should pick a different instrument," Namatame says. "So, I rented a set of drums and

I just told him, 'Play like you wanna play,' and he ended up being this incredible drummer. It was wild."

It was one of those all-ages shows at Seattle's Party Hall—a "weird little crusty punk place," Brock recalls—where he and Green first met through a mutual friend, the late Sam Jayne of Love as Laughter and Lync. "Jeremy had a weird sense of humor, we both did," Brock says. "When he was introduced to me, he leaned in and was like, 'You wanna fight?' I was like, 'No, I think not.'"

Within a few weeks, Green started jamming with Brock and Modest Mouse's original bassist, Eric Judy (who left the band in 2012), in a shed outside Brock's Issaquah home. "I loved what it was like to play music with Eric," Brock says. "Then when Jeremy came into the fold, it really truly just worked. It was [expletive] heaven."

As the youngest member of the band, Green had yet to complete high school when Modest Mouse went on its first of many tours over the next 25-plus years. "We lived together in close enough quarters for a long enough time that, in those scenarios you can go for a week in the same room and not need to have a meaningful conversation, you just joke," Brock says. "And that's not downplaying that, that's beautiful. Think about every time you've thought to yourself, you've been sitting in a room with someone, 'I need to say something.' I didn't need to say anything when I was around Jeremiah."

Modest Mouse released their first two albums on Seattle's Up Records, and as they gained traction in the late 1990s, the trio became one of the most prominent acts among a wave of bands that reaffirmed Seattle's place on the rock 'n' roll map after grunge's sunset. Modest Mouse reached greater commercial heights in the 2000s, starting with their major-label debut *The Moon & Antarctica*—one of the era's defining indie rock records that's often cited as their masterpiece.

In their early days, Modest Mouse had a reputation as a "feral" band (as Death Cab for Cutie's Ben Gibbard once affectionately put it), and according to friend and longtime Seattle DJ, Marco Collins, Green's steadying presence was a counterweight to the more "explosive" Brock, who would "turn into a different human being" on stage. "To me, [Green] was sort of the rudder of that band," says Collins, who bonded with Green over a shared love of electronic music. "He kept things on an even keel and maybe that dynamic between Jeremiah and Isaac made that band sort of work."

As Brock describes it, he relied on Green—the band's only other constant member, save for a brief hiatus around 2004's *Good News for People Who Love Bad News*—to "have his own vision this whole time so we wouldn't get stuck with like a monoculture" in the band.

"Jeremiah rarely actually played the same beat twice unless it was necessary," Brock says. "So, he managed to keep things new just because I don't think he wanted to do the same thing twice ever."

Beyond his Modest Mouse duties, Green stretched his creative wings with a number of other projects, including the post-punk quartet Satisfact and post-rockers Red Stars Theory in the late 1990s, and more recently Vells and his electro-washed World Gang. When not playing drums, Green often wrote electronic music and had his abstract eye behind a camera lens, posting some of his photos to his @sluglife Instagram handle. "He was wired that way to be creative every single day," says his brother, Adam.

Recently, Green had been sketching designs for an off-the-grid cabin he planned to build in Hawaii, where he was born while his father was in the Army. In true mossback fashion, he bought a plot of land on a particularly damp section of the island because he loved the rain.

"When he was going through chemo, he was super, super positive," Adam says. "Obviously, we thought that he was going to be fine, including him, so he had all these goals he wanted to do. He got kind of a second wind in life. He wanted to do all this traveling. He kept talking about how he could feel the breeze of Hawaii on his face. He wanted to go back there really, really bad; he couldn't wait."

To celebrate his birthday this weekend, Green's family planned a trip to Hawaii to scatter his ashes.

"One Foot in Front of the Next"

For years, Green had made his home in Port Townsend, a town that Namatame says truly embraced her son. Green, who was "kind of a woodsy guy" and not one for rock star indulgences, was a natural fit in the Olympic Peninsula outpost that boasts a vibrant artist community and offered a slower pace of life when he hopped off the tour bus. "I heard that now when they see somebody driving his pickup through town, that they cry," says Namatame, growing emotional, "because he was pretty special."

It was there Green started a family of his own with his wife, Lauren, and their six-year-old son, Wilder, who already owns more drum machines and audio samplers than most adults, Namatame says. "He told us all that someday he's going to be like his dad and play the drums, so we'll see."

After Green left the Modest Mouse tour last December, the band continued the run with drum tech Damon Cox on what was supposed to be a temporary fill-in basis. Modest Mouse is scheduled to play its first shows since Green's death later this month when the Lollapalooza festival heads to South America.

For now, Brock's taking a "one-foot-in-front-of-the-next" approach, still unsure how it will feel to lead the band into its next chapter without his childhood friend in the bunk across the tour bus aisle. "I imagine there's going to be a ghost in the house for quite a while," Brock says. "Not literally, but psychologically, we'll be looking at this through his lens on some level."

With Green's passing, Brock lost more than a "brother" and a creative partner of more than thirty years.

"I don't plan on speaking at his memorial," Brock said days before the February gathering. "I figure I'll just say this now." Brock went on to describe a "shared memory" he and Jeremiah had developed among their circle of friends. "We could tell each other stories about things that had happened in both of our lives and only one of us could remember. . . Sam Jayne, he remembered aspects of me and him and Jeremiah's life that lived only with him and when that was gone, that was gone. Jeremiah remembered parts of my life that I don't actually have the memory of, and so that's gone.

"That continues through the entire system, the entire web of friends, and the plus side to that [expletive] is this: All that stuff that Jeremiah didn't remember himself about his own life lives inside me, lives inside all the people that were around him. Those moments that you don't remember that other people do, you get to keep living in them. And that's the trick. That's it."[1]

[1]Republished with permission from *The Seattle Times*.

VI · XIII · MM

To quote *Wikipedia* (as of this writing): "*The Moon & Antarctica* is the third studio album by American rock band Modest Mouse, released on June 13, 2000, by Epic Records. The album's title is taken from the opening scene of the 1982 film *Blade Runner*, where the main character (Rick Deckard) reads a newspaper headlined 'Farming the Oceans, the Moon and Antarctica.'"

. . . Which was news to Isaac Brock when he first heard it a couple of years ago (and news to Judy when I told him about it during an interview for this book).

"Scouts honor," Brock says. "I'd seen *Blade Runner*. I just didn't ever bother reading what was on the fucking front page of that [newspaper]. It was a complete fucking accident. But once you know that, there's no unknowing it. And like, anyone who doesn't believe me—I absolutely understand. It's *pretty* random."

The real story behind the title: Brock says he doesn't know why, but he has always felt like the Moon and Antarctica are somehow connected; rather than cold, dead things, he sees them as spirits of sorts—neither evil nor good, they have an agreement.

"They're two characters in a fucking interesting story," he says. "There's just something so stark to both of them. That's part of what the handshake [on the cover of the record] is, just like two business hands—two hands that don't care about anything, making an agreement."

It wasn't supposed to be the title of the album, but: "How or why, I wish I could give you more, because you're writing a book. But the fact is, it was just the right thing. It got stuck in my head. It kind of came to fruition around the time that I felt like some entity had passed through me or latched on for a second. That's about when it showed up, and it just never went away, ever. It was what it was supposed to be."

When it came to visualizing that agreement on the cover of the record, the band turned to Welsh photographer Simon Larbalestier, best known for his work with the late 4AD designer Vaughan Oliver. Together, the pair had created the covers for the entire Pixies catalog—which Brock loved. So he gave Larbalestier a vague idea of what he was seeking, which included the handshake. But when he got the image back . . . it all just fell kind of flat for him. Given the trippy, if not surreal, Pixies covers Larbalestier had co-created, Brock was expecting something . . . more. (He did get his desired hue, though; Brock wanted the hands to be blue, inspired by the work of photographer Jan Saudek, who is known to color different elements of his monochromatic images to accentuate them, such as veins.)

While today Brock actually likes the cover—he stares at an image of it for a few moments and notes that vibe-wise, it's not too far off from *This Is a Long Drive for*

Someone with Nothing to Think About—a few years after its release, he would completely discard it. For a few years, anyway. Not to skip too far ahead, but while we're on the subject of album art, in 2004, Epic released a *Moon & Antarctica* reissue with new cover art, remastered audio, and four bonus tracks from a BBC studio session. This time around, Brock commissioned Matt Clark, who also created the cover for *Good News for People Who Love Bad News,* which would debut a month after the reissue. It's blue, utilizes the same Neue Helvetica typeface from the original, and perhaps makes an attempt to literally depict the Moon and Antarctica while also looking something like a Rorschach test. Brock liked it on screen. But, "When it was printed," especially at CD size, "I was like, 'What is this? What the fuck am I even looking at?' . . . I think it was a mountain. But there's maybe also a face or something. It was just a couple conversations, and it made perfect sense. And then once it was printed, I forgot what it was even supposed to be."

Brock says he felt high-maintenance asking the label for the reissue in the first place—and he says that it probably looked like a money grab. In reality, he was just dissatisfied with the cover and mastering. For the latter, the average listener probably can't even tell the difference (I reached out to Howie Weinberg, who remastered it, for some specifics, but did not hear back). In the end, Brock ended up reverting to the original art (but kept Weinberg's mastering) when Epic released the tenth-anniversary edition in 2010, which today stands as the most up-to-date iteration of the record.

Still, "I don't like the optics that I changed my mind on the cover. It shows a lack of commitment to the concept—and it was pretty close to the concept."

*   *   *

The original album, meanwhile, hit stores on June 13, 2000.

And scores of critics loved it.

At that point in time, Brock had a firm policy of not reading reviews. "I felt like any amount of paying attention to that sort of shit was going to somehow alter my process. And I didn't want my feelings about music to change based on other people's feelings about what I was doing. So I just assumed it didn't do very well."

If he *had* read the reviews, he'd have seen stuff like this:

The band's stunning major label debut—*The Moon and Antarctica*, a loosely based concept album about lost identity and isolation—is the perfect drug. It makes your teeth whiter, your thoughts deeper and your waistline thinner. One listen to epic alt-rock track "The Stars Are Projectors," or slap-dash hit "Gravity Rides Everything," and you'll feel 10 years younger and 10 times richer. It will restore your faith in the power of alternative rock and the electric guitar. (Christopher Waters, *The Standard*)

You officially have not heard Modest Mouse until you have heard their major label debut. . . . An intoxicating mix of uncertainty and confidence, *The Moon & Antarctica* constructs hallow approximations of heaven, hell and deep space—most of which exist vividly in

Isaac Brock's questioning mind. *OK Computer* must be mentioned, for Modest Mouse just got invited to the same club. They can chat existentially in the sauna. But unlike Radiohead's unease at technology and quickening society, Modest Mouse grapple with the general conjectures of humankind. The title aptly entails the whole of the album. Sometimes the most spooky, alien places are not too far off. Similarly, our immediate surroundings and internal environment feel even more otherworldly. Modest Mouse seek salvation in God, death and relationships. Fortunately, the rest of us can sometimes find it in records. (Brent DiCrescenzo, *Pitchfork*)

Of course, not everyone can hang. Notably, *The New York Times*, which wrote in a show preview, "Its recent major label debut, *The Moon and Antarctica* (Epic), lost it some credibility, perhaps because of its less-chaotic sound."

And Ben Massarella says that very notion, in fact, was a real fear among those who worked on the record: *Would longtime fans hate it because it greatly expanded on the band's signature trio approach to that point?* He was thrilled when fans seemed to side, instead, with the critics.

For his part, Brock had a creeping suspicion that the alternative and indie world was going to pass on it because Modest Mouse had signed with Epic—and were therefore no longer sanctified. ("I am embarrassed to say that I even made concessions for anything, which is to say, I definitely steered away from going too pop," he adds.)

Personally, he loved what the band had created . . . but he says he doesn't think Epic had any idea what to do with it.

When he brought the band to the label, Matt Marshall says his goal was to not oversell them; given that Modest Mouse's financial deal wasn't in the league of, say, a Pearl Jam or Celine Dion at the time, they flew a bit under the radar. "Perhaps a little naive," Marshall thus hoped the music and results would speak for themselves. He was also crossing his fingers that the record would sell around 5,000 copies or so on release (by comparison, at his first label, Zoo, he says 2,000 would have been considered a fantastic start out of the gate). He doesn't remember the exact number but estimates that *The Moon & Antarctica* sold between 13,000 and 15,000 copies in its first week, blowing past his expectations. He adored the record and was over the moon.

"I was like, 'Oh my God, this is exciting. Let's go after radio. Let's make a video.' And the head of the label called me up and she said, 'Yeah, that's a nice first week.' And I said, 'Great. Can we go after a track at radio?' And she said, 'Honey, please, when they get to 50,000, call me.'"

So when they got to 50,000, he did. And he quickly found himself in the mire of major-label politics. He lobbied, and he lobbied hard—but he says that ultimately he was told to cool it because he was jeopardizing his job, and they weren't going to do it. There would be no radio. No video.[1]

---

[1]At the time, actor and director Vincent Gallo was riding high from his film *Buffalo '66*—and Marshall says he wanted to make a music video for the band. But the label refused to pony up the cash for it. "Don't get me wrong, it might have been an art piece that would have been a waste of money, or it might have been awesome," Marshall says, "but I still dream about what Vincent Gallo might have done."

"And I was like, I don't understand—this is something that's working," he says.

Per Marshall, it all led to a tough phone call with Brock. "[Isaac said,] 'We signed with a major to go after radio, make a video—and we got to do neither.' And there was nothing I could say other than, 'You know, I'm as surprised as you are.'"

As *The Salt Lake Tribune* quoted Brock at the time, "'You have to hire some promotions person to talk to the radio stations, and you have to pay this certain promotion company to push a song,' Brock said, emphasizing his words to underscore how exasperating the process is. 'That's why there's a bunch of crap on the radio. Epic's not even going to bother trying to put us on the radio, just because—and I'm quoting someone who was quoting someone at Epic— there's nothing else out there that sounds like us, so it would be really risky to put us on the radio.'"

Even without the support of those assets, Marshall says the record ended up selling a couple hundred thousand copies and "really built them stronger, such that when *Good News* came out, they were really poised to explode—which is obviously in retrospect what happened."

Though he had already left Epic for a different label by the time of *Good News*' release, in that moment—which disproved the whispered theory that the best a band like Modest Mouse could ever do was sell a couple hundred thousand copies—Marshall says he indeed felt vindicated.

For a moment, Brock also had cinematic aspirations—he had pondered making a *Moon & Antarctica* movie. ("I'm trying to remember what the premise of the fucking *Moon & Antarctica* movie even was. That's how much that died on the vine.") Today, he's thankful he didn't. And ironically, he's also thankful no *Moon & Antarctica* music videos got made, either—"I think that can kind of seal the fate of a song in someone's mind; it can never be anything more than those visuals. And so if I'd come out with an entire poorly, or even well-conceived, David Lynch movie for that record, it would have taken too much ownership in people's minds, and it wouldn't get to belong to them. And I think that's one of the reasons that that record still does OK, is no one's picturing me as a fucking old sailor with a fucking fake hand," he says, referencing the sea-shanty video for "Dashboard," "which was really fun, looked great, but had *nothing* to do with fucking anything on the song."

Though no one wanted it at the time, the record would ultimately go on to speak for itself.

Aftermath

The Moon & Antarctica peaked at No. 120 on the Billboard 200 chart . . . and then disappeared from it. By comparison, Modest Mouse's most commercially successful albums would go on to include *Good News for People Who Love Bad News*, which charted for fifty-seven weeks and peaked at No. 18, and *We Were Dead Before the Ship Even Sank*, which charted for twenty-five weeks and peaked at No. 1.

Modest Mouse is still very much active, having released *The Golden Casket* in 2021, constantly touring, and even playing a halftime show at a Seattle Seahawks game in 2023. Perhaps the key to the band's enduring longevity: "If you like a pretty song like '3rd Planet,' oftentimes, you're not going to want to hear the 'water and shit' song ['What People Are Made Of']," Isaac Brock says. "I've found it interesting that we've found enough people who actually generally like both songs."

In retrospect, *The Moon & Antarctica* represents an inflection point for Modest Mouse. Music critic Jordan Bassett says the songwriting, production, and thematic elements were a "quantum leap" forward for the trio—and it showcased a band that had fully come to fruition. For Eric

Judy, the record marked a bit of an end to the first chapter of the group and the start of another. Indeed, with *Good News* and the subsequent releases, the band would grow in size, scope, visibility, fame, and Johnny Marr.

From a songwriting perspective, Brock says that after *The Moon & Antarctica*, he tried to loosen his grip on the creative process a bit and be less of a musical autocrat. As for those tunes that would follow, I'd long guessed that the sprawling arrangements of the record had instilled in him a desire to write simpler tracks—but true to his initial warning that I'd get different answers to my queries on different days, Brock initially agreed . . . but then a few months later had reconsidered. (Either way, "Writing a non-pandering pop song isn't fucking particularly easy," Brock says. He adds that he knew he was making a pop record with *Good News*—"but I didn't think I was making *that* poppy a record.")

And in fact, when he wrote the songs that would appear on *Good News* and turned the record in, he did so with the full assumption that the label was going to drop Modest Mouse. Matt Marshall was gone, and Brock says no one at Epic even knew who they were. He adds that it was a fluke that *Good News* got any attention at all and that it happened when the label's president was throwing a temper tantrum and lamenting that they didn't have anything good in the pipeline—and someone who had a copy of the record piped up and put it on, and he said, "That's it!"

. . . However, per Brock, the executive's recollection was that the band had turned the album in, and he bemoaned to them that it did not have a hit on it and demanded they not come back until they had written one. And thus Brock returned with "Float On" in hand.

"That did not happen," Brock deadpans.

While *The Moon & Antarctica* did not achieve the financial and commercial windfall that *Good News* did (if only the president of Epic had demanded a single), it did reverberate throughout the industry in intriguing ways.

Today, hearing indie artists in, say, Apple commercials, is *de rigueur*. But at the turn of the millennium, Marshall says Modest Mouse was one of two key bands that made licensing music palatable, the other being The Verve and its "Bitter Sweet Symphony" Nike commercial. When Brock planted his flag and delivered his rant on integrity (as he recapped earlier in this book, "If I'm doing something I enjoy and I'm making money and things and I use my art to make money . . . don't question my integrity, because where's my integrity when I'm washing dishes for minimum wage or selling fucking plasma or whatever?"), Marshall says people took notice. "The majority of the indie scene was like, 'You know what? He's damn right.' . . . I think that was a sea change in the industry."

As others have written, the record would go on to help dispel the precious notion that by signing to a major label, you were also signing away not just the quality, originality, and independence of your output but your fanbase as well. A more predictable scenario might have seen Modest Mouse releasing *Good News* as their major-label debut, ostracizing fans who were subconsciously seeking ostracization, and then following it with *The Moon & Antarctica* as a reactionary album and getting dropped by the label. Instead, thanks to Brock's approach to the album, luck, and perhaps the fact that Epic forgot about the strange little band flying under the radar, Modest Mouse endures. (And in the process, Marshall adds, "I had a lot of friends who were musicians who said 'Modest Mouse just changed radio and changed a lot of things.' I think they opened the door for a lot of the indie artists that broke through afterwards.")

Weirdness went mainstream—and the world is that much better for it (or at least that much more interesting).

What is the record's ultimate legacy—and where can we see it today?

To Brock's earlier point about radio, perhaps nowhere. And perhaps *that* is its legacy.

"It's a massively underrated record," Bassett says. "People should talk about in the same breath as a record like *Kid A*. If you're talking about a record that is thematically consistent, that is wildly, wildly ambitious . . . I mean, it's one of the most ambitious albums I've ever heard. There are some great tunes on it that are really, really distinctive and unique—and I don't think *anything* sounds like this. It's so hard to be original in music, especially as a rock band that plays with guitars. And there's never been any record that sounds like this—since or before."

As the sun begins to sag in the Portland sky, someone swings by to pick up an electric motorcycle that Brock rode in Los Angeles during the recording of *The Golden Casket*. Only problem is, "I kept crashing it," he says as he turns it on. "People my age with fucking kids shouldn't get motorcycles. Until they figure out a way to build a shell that encompasses

the entire thing, and maybe put four wheels instead of just two
. . . until they come up with that, I'm not riding motorcycles."

Brock warns his visitor about the lightning-fast electric pickup and momentarily glides around Ice Cream Party as taxidermied ducks, a mannequin wearing pelts, and a giant rabbit-costume head look on.

I don't know but I been told, you never die and you never grow old

I don't know but I been told—

I think that technically counts as saying you'll never die.

Coda

The next day, Isaac Brock appears at Ice Cream Party seemingly refreshed—perhaps because I told him I only needed about forty more minutes of his time to go over a few remaining questions.

"I wasn't too drunk for you last night, was I?" he asks.

Not at all. While tales of wild Brock antics abound, once the motorcycle was offloaded, the rest of the day entailed listening to music, everything from new unreleased Modest Mouse songs to Brock's favorite local musician who plays the same bar every Friday.

After I've run out of questions, we decide to grab lunch.

"Do you want Burmese, Indian, or Japanese?" he asks.

Having never had Burmese food, I say Indian or Japanese.

Brock thinks for a moment. "I think you made the wrong choice," he says. "I gave you three choices. And only one was right."

At the Burmese joint down the street, the server takes our drink order—but rather than alcohol, we both opt for Burmese iced tea, which arrives in a tall glass with whipped cream and a yellow and white paper straw. It's either a delightful contrast or complement to Brock's kaleidoscopic mushroom shirt and heavily tattooed arms—perhaps a study in extremes, not entirely unlike *The Moon & Antarctica*, which Brock seems utterly relieved to finally be free of discussing.

As I sip the tea, I ponder his observation that observing songs changes them. And I consider the very real possibility that this book could ruin *The Moon & Antarctica* for some readers. When chatting about "I Came as a Rat" yesterday, Brock noted how discussing the inspiration behind music oversimplifies or makes frivolous work of inspired moments.

> It seems to me like maybe the reason that music works at all for everyone—why it's ever worked—is its lack of being specific. . . . I'm just kind of making this up right now as I go along, but I think that it's the link between raw emotions or the electricity in your brain firing off to make a thought prior to it becoming something that you can really look at. It's somewhere in between all this shit. It's like right before you fall asleep—you know when you feel like you're about to step off something and you jolt? It's *that* moment.

He continued,

> It's not just pure fucking dumb animal fluids. And it's not, you know, like Greek philosopher–like focus. It's that messy shit that is most of our fucking lives. . . . And that's the least cop-out-y way I can explain why I don't like explaining songs. Why I don't actually think that it does the songs any justice. And why I think that I'm lying when

I give answers to what songs are about. Because they're not generally about anything except for that fucking moment in time or that feeling you have about something that you can't yet identify. . . . I mean, I kind of half-expected if the hypnotism had worked, that the answers would be so fucking boring, it would have been pointless anyways.

Prior to that session, I gave the hypnotist some background—Isaac Brock was a musician, and he was having trouble remembering the recording of a particular album.

"But why is that so important? Remembering that?" she asked.

Hell. Maybe it wasn't in the end, after all.

Appendix

Quick Guide to the People Mentioned in This Book

- Isaac Brock: Founding Modest Mouse (and Ugly Casanova) songwriter, singer, guitarist, multi-instrumentalist
- Eric Judy: Founding Modest Mouse bassist, multi-instrumentalist
- Jeremiah Green (1977–2022): Founding Modest Mouse drummer
- Brian Deck: Producer; former member of Red Red Meat and Ugly Casanova; Califone collaborator
- Matt Marshall: A&R rep
- Ben Massarella: Percussionist, member of Modest Mouse; former member of Red Red Meat; Califone collaborator
- Tim Rutili: Founder of Califone and Red Red Meat; former member of Ugly Casanova
- Greg Ratajczak: Former Clava Studios intern and later studio assistant
- Jordan Bassett: Music journalist; former commissioning editor, *NME*

Partial Modest Mouse Discography

Studio Albums

- *This Is a Long Drive for Someone with Nothing to Think About* (Up Records, 1996)
- *The Lonesome Crowded West* (Up Records, 1997)
- *The Moon & Antarctica* (Epic, 2000)
- *Good News for People Who Love Bad News* (Epic, 2004)
- *We Were Dead Before the Ship Even Sank* (Epic, 2007)
- *Strangers to Ourselves* (Epic, 2015)
- *The Golden Casket* (Epic, 2021)

Other Releases

- *Building Nothing Out of Something* (Up Records, 2000, compilation)
- *Sad Sappy Sucker* (K Records, 2001, anomaly/curiosity)

EPs

- *Blue Cadet-3, Do You Connect?* (K Records, 1994)
- *Interstate 8* (Up Records, 1996)

- *The Fruit That Ate Itself* (K Records, 1997)
- *Night on the Sun* (Up Records, 2000)
- *Everywhere and His Nasty Parlour Tricks* (Epic, 2001)
- *No One's First, and You're Next* (Epic, 2009)

Bibliography

Front of Book

Tim McMahon, "Modest Mouse: Running with the Devil," *The Reader*, October 15, 1998, http://www.timmcmahan.com/modest1.htm/.

By Way of Introduction: Fuck You, Cowboy

Brent DiCrescenzo, "The Moon & Antarctica," *Pitchfork,* June 13, 2000, http://pitchfork.com/reviews/albums/5358-the-moon-antarctica/.

Jordan Bassett, "Modest Mouse—'The Golden Casket' Review: The Spiritual Sequel to their Breakout Hit," *NME*, June 22, 2021, http://www.nme.com/reviews/modest-mouse-the-golden-casket-review-2972977/.

Steven Hyden, "Modest Mouse's 'The Moon & Antarctica' Shaped 21st Century Indie Rock," *Uproxx*, June 8, 2020, http://uproxx.com/indie/modest-mouse-moon-and-antarctica-20th-anniversary/.

Building Nothing Out of Something

Frank Mullen, "Isaac Brock Interview," *Ink 19,* November 9, 1998,
    http://ink19.com/1998/11/magazine/interviews/xjcfsr-modest
    -mouse/.
Jon Ferguson, "Not to Brag, But . . . Modest Mouse May have
    a Major-label Budget Now, But They Haven't Sold Out,"
    Intelligencer Journal, May 12, 2000, 2.
Mark Richardson, "There's a Star Above the Manger Tonight,"
    Pitchfork, January 15, 2015, http://pitchfork.com/reviews/
    albums/19948-theres-a-star-above-the-manger-tonight/.
Tim McMahon, "Modest Mouse: Running with the Devil," *The
    Reader*, October 15, 1998, http://www.timmcmahan.com/
    modest1.htm/.

The Devil's Apprentice

"Modest Mouse Insist Major-Label Deal Changes Nothing," *MTV*,
    June 26, 2000, http://www.mtv.com/news/efcbyu/modest
    -mouse-insist-major-label-deal-changes-nothing/.
Virginia Woolf, "The Mark on the Wall" in *Monday or Tuesday*
    (New York: Harcourt, Brace and Company Inc., 1921), 99–116.

Emptying the Bottle

Bob Susnjara, "Comiskey Park Neighbors Come to Bat for Area
    Owner of Popular Bar, Patrons Say Bridgeport's a 'Nice, homey
    place,'" *Daily Herald*, October 4, 2000, 14.
John G. Raffensperger, *The Old Lady on Harrison Street: Cook County
    Hospital, 1833–1995* (New York: Peter Lang Publishing, 1997).

"Modest Mouse / SUDSY MALONE'S CINCINNATI, OHIO 1997-11-08," August 23, 2023, http://www.youtube.com/watch?v=IsVV6QETMzg/.

Rick Weldon, "The Making of the Moon," *Electronic Musician*, January 2001, Vol. 17, Issue 1, 114.

Aside: *Everywhere and His Nasty Parlour Tricks*

Douglas Wolk, "Everywhere and His Nasty Parlour Tricks," *Rolling Stone,* December 6, 2001, 149.

Mark Brown, "Mouse's Output No Modest Sum; New EP Proves That Even Band's Castoff Songs Are Keepers," *Rocky Mountain News*, October 10, 2001, 13D.

Tom Scanlon, "Indie Rock's Chris Takino Pioneered Industry Trends," *The Seattle Times*, October 19, 2000, http://archive.seattletimes.com/archive/?date=20001019&slug=4048633/.

The Moon & Antarctica

Cormac McCarthy, *Blood Meridian* (New York: Vintage, 1992), 330–5. http://www.adforum.com/creative-work/ad/player/36261/moms-have-changed/nissan/.

JC Gabel, "Q&A: Isaac Brock of Modest Mouse," *Stop Smiling,* December 9, 2007, http://stopsmilingonline.com/story_detail.php?id=935/.

Jonathan Valania, "Modest Mouse's Isaac Brock Wants To Be More Than A Myth," *BuzzFeed*, March 30, 2015, http://www.buzzfeed.com/jonathanvalania/modest-mouses-isaac-brock-wants-to-be-more-than-a-myth/.

Josh Modell, "Modest Mouse," *The AV Club*, April 7, 2004, http://www.avclub.com/modest-mouse-1798208359/.

Letters to the Editor, *The Stranger*, April 1, 1999, http://www.thestranger.com/columns/1999/04/01/618/letters-to-the-editor/.

Nathalie Claeys, "Modest Mouse," *KindaMuzik*, December 3, 2000, http://www.kindamuzik.net/interview/modest-mouse/modest-mouse/395/index.html/.

Ryan Schreiber, "Modest Mouse," *Pitchfork*, September, 1996, http://web.archive.org/web/20010701222355/http://pitchforkmedia.com/interviews/m/modest-mouse-96/.

Rick Weldon, "The Making of the Moon," *Electronic Musician*, January 2001, Vol. 17, Issue 1, 114.

Ryan Leas, "We've Got a File On You: Johnny Marr," *Stereogum*, October 13, 2021, http://www.stereogum.com/2163778/johnny-marr-the-smiths-noel-gallagher-modest-mouse-hans-zimmer/interviews/weve-got-a-file-on-you/.

Samantha M. Shapiro, "Immodest Mouse," *The Stranger*, March 18, 1999.

Tim McMahon, "Modest Mouse: Running with the Devil," *The Reader*, October 15, 1998, http://www.timmcmahan.com/modest1.htm/.

Tom Scanlon, "Man or Mouse? Isaac Brock Takes a Pop (Rock) Quiz," *Seattle Times*, June 11, 2002, http://archive.seattletimes.com/archive/?date=20020611&slug=brock11/.

Aside: Jeremiah Green

Michael Rietmulder, "Remembering Jeremiah Green, Modest Mouse's Soft-spoken 'Rudder'," *The Seattle Times,* March 1, 2023, http://www.seattletimes.com/entertainment/music/remembering-jeremiah-green-modest-mouses-soft-spoken-rudder/.

VI · XIII · MM

Brent DiCrescenzo, "The Moon & Antarctica," *Pitchfork,* June 13, 2000, http://pitchfork.com/reviews/albums/5358-the-moon -antarctica/.

Christopher Waters, "Music That Matters," *The Standard*, January 6, 2001, E2.

Dan Nailen, "Modest Mouse Too Mighty for Today's Radio," *The Salt Lake Tribune*, September 8, 2000, E12.

Acknowledgments

With love to M. Z.; S. P.; M. P.; R. P.; B. W.; S. N.; and those amazing people in my life when I first heard these songs, who are inextricably steeped within them: G. L.; C. O. B.; E. F.; D. D.; and M. W.

And with perpetual thanks to Leah Babb-Rosenfeld, Ryan Pinkard, and Matthew Sadie for their critical roles in making this book happen.

Also Available in the Series

1. *Dusty Springfield's Dusty in Memphis* by Warren Zanes
2. *Love's Forever Changes* by Andrew Hultkrans
3. *Neil Young's Harvest* by Sam Inglis
4. *The Kinks' The Kinks Are the Village Green Preservation Society* by Andy Miller
5. *The Smiths' Meat Is Murder* by Joe Pernice
6. *Pink Floyd's The Piper at the Gates of Dawn* by John Cavanagh
7. *ABBA's ABBA Gold: Greatest Hits* by Elisabeth Vincentelli
8. *The Jimi Hendrix Experience's Electric Ladyland* by John Perry
9. *Joy Division's Unknown Pleasures* by Chris Ott
10. *Prince's Sign "☮" the Times* by Michaelangelo Matos
11. *The Velvet Underground's The Velvet Underground & Nico* by Joe Harvard
12. *The Beatles' Let It Be* by Steve Matteo
13. *James Brown's Live at the Apollo* by Douglas Wolk
14. *Jethro Tull's Aqualung* by Allan Moore
15. *Radiohead's OK Computer* by Dai Griffiths
16. *The Replacements' Let It Be* by Colin Meloy
17. *Led Zeppelin's Led Zeppelin IV* by Erik Davis
18. *The Rolling Stones' Exile on Main St.* by Bill Janovitz
19. *The Beach Boys' Pet Sounds* by Jim Fusilli
20. *Ramones' Ramones* by Nicholas Rombes
21. *Elvis Costello's Armed Forces* by Franklin Bruno
22. *R.E.M.'s Murmur* by J. Niimi

23. *Jeff Buckley's Grace* by Daphne Brooks

24. *DJ Shadow's Endtroducing . . .* by Eliot Wilder

25. *MC5's Kick Out the Jams* by Don McLeese

26. *David Bowie's Low* by Hugo Wilcken

27. *Bruce Springsteen's Born in the U.S.A.* by Geoffrey Himes

28. *The Band's Music from Big Pink* by John Niven

29. *Neutral Milk Hotel's In the Aeroplane over the Sea* by Kim Cooper

30. *Beastie Boys' Paul's Boutique* by Dan Le Roy

31. *Pixies' Doolittle* by Ben Sisario

32. *Sly and the Family Stone's There's a Riot Goin' On* by Miles Marshall Lewis

33. *The Stone Roses' The Stone Roses* by Alex Green

34. *Nirvana's In Utero* by Gillian G. Gaar

35. *Bob Dylan's Highway 61 Revisited* by Mark Polizzotti

36. *My Bloody Valentine's Loveless* by Mike McGonigal

37. *The Who's The Who Sell Out* by John Dougan

38. *Guided by Voices' Bee Thousand* by Marc Woodworth

39. *Sonic Youth's Daydream Nation* by Matthew Stearns

40. *Joni Mitchell's Court and Spark* by Sean Nelson

41. *Guns N' Roses' Use Your Illusion I and II* by Eric Weisbard

42. *Stevie Wonder's Songs in the Key of Life* by Zeth Lundy

43. *The Byrds' The Notorious Byrd Brothers* by Ric Menck

44. *Captain Beefheart's Trout Mask Replica* by Kevin Courrier

45. *Minutemen's Double Nickels on the Dime* by Michael T. Fournier

46. *Steely Dan's Aja* by Don Breithaupt

47. *A Tribe Called Quest's People's Instinctive Travels and the Paths of Rhythm* by Shawn Taylor

48. *PJ Harvey's Rid of Me* by Kate Schatz

49. *U2's Achtung Baby* by Stephen Catanzarite

50. *Belle & Sebastian's If You're Feeling Sinister* by Scott Plagenhoef

51. *Nick Drake's Pink Moon* by Amanda Petrusich

52. *Celine Dion's Let's Talk About Love* by Carl Wilson

53. *Tom Waits' Swordfishtrombones* by David Smay

54. *Throbbing Gristle's 20 Jazz Funk Greats* by Drew Daniel

55. *Patti Smith's Horses* by Philip Shaw

56. *Black Sabbath's Master of Reality* by John Darnielle

57. *Slayer's Reign in Blood* by D. X. Ferris

58. *Richard and Linda Thompson's Shoot Out the Lights* by Hayden Childs

59. *The Afghan Whigs' Gentlemen* by Bob Gendron

60. *The Pogues' Rum, Sodomy, and the Lash* by Jeffery T. Roesgen

61. *The Flying Burrito Brothers' The Gilded Palace of Sin* by Bob Proehl

62. *Wire's Pink Flag* by Wilson Neate

63. *Elliott Smith's XO* by Mathew Lemay

64. *Nas' Illmatic* by Matthew Gasteier

65. *Big Star's Radio City* by Bruce Eaton

66. *Madness' One Step Beyond . . .* by Terry Edwards

67. *Brian Eno's Another Green World* by Geeta Dayal

68. *The Flaming Lips' Zaireeka* by Mark Richardson

69. *The Magnetic Fields' 69 Love Songs* by LD Beghtol

70. *Israel Kamakawiwo'ole's Facing Future* by Dan Kois

71. *Public Enemy's It Takes a Nation of Millions to Hold Us Back* by Christopher R. Weingarten

72. *Pavement's Wowee Zowee* by Bryan Charles

73. *AC/DC's Highway to Hell* by Joe Bonomo

74. *Van Dyke Parks's Song Cycle* by Richard Henderson

75. *Slint's Spiderland* by Scott Tennent

76. *Radiohead's Kid A* by Marvin Lin

77. *Fleetwood Mac's Tusk* by Rob Trucks

78. *Nine Inch Nails' Pretty Hate Machine* by Daphne Carr

79. *Ween's Chocolate and Cheese* by Hank Shteamer

80. *Johnny Cash's American Recordings* by Tony Tost

81. *The Rolling Stones' Some Girls* by Cyrus Patell

82. *Dinosaur Jr.'s You're Living All Over Me* by Nick Attfield

83. *Television's Marquee Moon* by Bryan Waterman

84. *Aretha Franklin's Amazing Grace* by Aaron Cohen

85. *Portishead's Dummy* by RJ Wheaton

86. *Talking Heads' Fear of Music* by Jonathan Lethem

87. *Serge Gainsbourg's Histoire de Melody Nelson* by Darran Anderson

88. *They Might Be Giants' Flood* by S. Alexander Reed and Elizabeth Sandifer

89. *Andrew W. K.'s I Get Wet* by Phillip Crandall

90. *Aphex Twin's Selected Ambient Works Volume II* by Marc Weidenbaum

91. *Gang of Four's Entertainment* by Kevin J. H. Dettmar

92. *Richard Hell and the Voidoids' Blank Generation* by Pete Astor

93. *J Dilla's Donuts* by Jordan Ferguson

94. *The Beach Boys' Smile* by Luis Sanchez

95. *Oasis' Definitely Maybe* by Alex Niven

96. *Liz Phair's Exile in Guyville* by Gina Arnold

97. *Kanye West's My Beautiful Dark Twisted Fantasy* by Kirk Walker Graves

98. *Danger Mouse's The Grey Album* by Charles Fairchild

99. *Sigur Rós's ()* by Ethan Hayden

100. *Michael Jackson's Dangerous* by Susan Fast

101. *Can's Tago Mago* by Alan Warner

102. *Bobbie Gentry's Ode to Billie Joe* by Tara Murtha

103. *Hole's Live Through This* by Anwen Crawford

104. *Devo's Freedom of Choice* by Evie Nagy

105. *Dead Kennedys' Fresh Fruit for Rotting Vegetables* by Michael Stewart Foley

106. *Koji Kondo's Super Mario Bros.* by Andrew Schartmann

107. *Beat Happening's Beat Happening* by Bryan C. Parker

108. *Metallica's Metallica* by David Masciotra

109. *Phish's A Live One* by Walter Holland

110. *Miles Davis' Bitches Brew* by George Grella Jr.

111. *Blondie's Parallel Lines* by Kembrew McLeod

112. *Grateful Dead's Workingman's Dead* by Buzz Poole

113. *New Kids On The Block's Hangin' Tough* by Rebecca Wallwork

114. *The Geto Boys' The Geto Boys* by Rolf Potts

115. *Sleater-Kinney's Dig Me Out* by Jovana Babovic

116. *LCD Soundsystem's Sound of Silver* by Ryan Leas

117. *Donny Hathaway's Donny Hathaway Live* by Emily J. Lordi

118. *The Jesus and Mary Chain's Psychocandy* by Paula Mejia

119. *The Modern Lovers' The Modern Lovers* by Sean L. Maloney

120. *Angelo Badalamenti's Soundtrack from Twin Peaks* by Clare Nina Norelli

121. *Young Marble Giants' Colossal Youth* by Michael Blair and Joe Bucciero

122. *The Pharcyde's Bizarre Ride II the Pharcyde* by Andrew Barker

123. *Arcade Fire's The Suburbs* by Eric Eidelstein

124. *Bob Mould's Workbook* by Walter Biggins and Daniel Couch

125. *Camp Lo's Uptown Saturday Night* by Patrick Rivers and Will Fulton

126. *The Raincoats' The Raincoats* by Jenn Pelly

127. *Björk's Homogenic* by Emily Mackay

128. *Merle Haggard's Okie from Muskogee* by Rachel Lee Rubin

129. *Fugazi's In on the Kill Taker* by Joe Gross

130. *Jawbreaker's 24 Hour Revenge Therapy* by Ronen Givony

131. *Lou Reed's Transformer* by Ezra Furman

132. *Siouxsie and the Banshees' Peepshow* by Samantha Bennett

133. *Drive-By Truckers' Southern Rock Opera* by Rien Fertel

134. *dc Talk's Jesus Freak* by Will Stockton and D. Gilson

135. *Tori Amos's Boys for Pele* by Amy Gentry

136. *Odetta's One Grain of Sand* by Matthew Frye Jacobson

137. *Manic Street Preachers' The Holy Bible* by David Evans

138. *The Shangri-Las' Golden Hits of the Shangri-Las* by Ada Wolin

139. *Tom Petty's Southern Accents* by Michael Washburn

140. *Massive Attack's Blue Lines* by Ian Bourland

141. *Wendy Carlos's Switched-On Bach* by Roshanak Kheshti

142. *The Wild Tchoupitoulas' The Wild Tchoupitoulas* by Bryan Wagner

143. *David Bowie's Diamond Dogs* by Glenn Hendler

144. *D'Angelo's Voodoo* by Faith A. Pennick

145. *Judy Garland's Judy at Carnegie Hall* by Manuel Betancourt

146. *Elton John's Blue Moves* by Matthew Restall

147. *Various Artists' I'm Your Fan: The Songs of Leonard Cohen* by Ray Padgett

148. *Janet Jackson's The Velvet Rope* by Ayanna Dozier

149. *Suicide's Suicide* by Andi Coulter

150. *Elvis Presley's From Elvis in Memphis* by Eric Wolfson

151. *Nick Cave and the Bad Seeds' Murder Ballads* by Santi Elijah Holley

152. *24 Carat Black's Ghetto: Misfortune's Wealth* by Zach Schonfeld

153. *Carole King's Tapestry* by Loren Glass

154. *Pearl Jam's Vs.* by Clint Brownlee

155. *Roxy Music's Avalon* by Simon Morrison

156. *Duran Duran's Rio* by Annie Zaleski

157. *Donna Summer's Once Upon a Time* by Alex Jeffery

158. *Sam Cooke's Live at the Harlem Square Club, 1963* by Colin Fleming

159. *Janelle Monáe's The ArchAndroid* by Alyssa Favreau

160. *John Prine's John Prine* by Erin Osmon

161. *Maria Callas's Lyric and Coloratura Arias* by Ginger Dellenbaugh

162. *The National's Boxer* by Ryan Pinkard

163. *Kraftwerk's Computer World* by Steve Tupai Francis

164. *Cat Power's Moon Pix* by Donna Kozloskie

165. *George Michael's Faith* by Matthew Horton

166. *Kendrick Lamar's To Pimp a Butterfly* by Sequoia Maner

167. *Britney Spears's Blackout* by Natasha Lasky

168. *Earth, Wind & Fire's That's the Way of the World* by Dwight E. Brooks

169. *Minnie Riperton's Come to My Garden* by Brittnay L. Proctor

170. *Babes in Toyland's Fontanelle* by Selena Chambers

171. *Madvillain's Madvillainy* by Will Hagle

172. *ESG's Come Away with ESG* by Cheri Percy

173. *BBC Radiophonic Workshop's BBC Radiophonic Workshop: A Retrospective* by William Weir

174. *Living Colour's Time's Up* by Kimberly Mack

175. *The Go-Go's Beauty and the Beat* by Lisa Whittington-Hill

176. *Madonna's Erotica* by Michael Dango

177. *Body Count's Body Count* by Ben Apatoff

178. *k.d. lang's Ingénue* by Joanna McNaney Stein

179. *Little Richard's Here's Little Richard* by Jordan Bassett

180. *Cardi B's Invasion of Privacy* by Ma'Chell Duma

181. *Pulp's This Is Hardcore* by Jane Savidge

182. *The Clash's Sandinista!* by Micajah Henley

183. *Depeche Mode's 101* by Mary Valle

184. *The Isley Brothers' 3+3* by Darrell M. McNeill

185. *Various Artists' Red Hot + Blue* by John S. Garrison

186. *Dolly Parton's White Limozeen* by Steacy Easton

187. *Garth Brooks' In the Life of Chris Gaines* by Stephen Deusner

188. *Kate Bush's Hounds of Love* by Leah Kardos